# the devil's monologue

### a.e. hepburn

TATE PUBLISHING, LLC

Published in the United States of America
by Tate Publishing, LLC
127 East Trade Center Terrace
Mustang, OK 73064
(888) 361–9473

ISBN: 1–5988601–7-8

*Dedicated to my brother, Michael,*
*who sleeps with the angels.*

# INTRODUCTION

Let me tell you what happens in a place where demons congregate. The forces of hell meet in places where even angels avoid going, in active volcanoes, burial grounds, the darkest parts of the oceans, the hottest spots in deserts, and on desolate planets. Our meetings are always chaotic. Spirits of jealously and their cohorts, imps that perpetrate envy and strife, are forever attempting to undermine my authority!

Every evening at the end of the Sabbath, my hordes and I congregate to strategize modes of destruction aimed at humankind. The assembly of evil spirits is enough to make even the toughest of human lose his lunch, his ability to speak, and control of his vital organs. The hideous faces, gruesome, monstrous bodies of the demonic horde in attendance are so horrific that even the most horrendous of demons tremble as the repugnant creatures stroll in one after the other to assemble for a satanic conclave. The stench that accompanies the malevolent force is a combination of brimstone and sulfur, rotting carcasses fit for carrion, the scent of burning flesh mixed with animal puke and human excrement. The atmosphere is thick with iniquity. Violence, anger, hatred, jealousy, murder, envy, strife, lust, and lasciviousness permeate the atmosphere.

Always present at these gatherings are the most popular of demons—Despair in its small, slithery serpentine form, and its associate, Doubt, a boney, gaunt, beaked creature with bibulous bulging eyes and spidery webbed wings. Doubt and Despair are two demon powers that I find to be productive in my campaign to thwart the force of goodness. The strongman is always present at my gatherings along with his numerous imps that bring about human addictions. Spirits representing deceit, strife, and greed are applauded by the hounds of hell. However, the demons that represent inner rottenness—hatred and lawlessness—spirits directing these vices are hell's favorite.

My position as prince over the power of darkness is challenged at every meeting because there is no loyalty among demons.

# CHAPTER I

Who am I? An angel.

What am I? A devil.

How old am I? Ageless, or at least that is what I want you to believe.

So I think I will begin this monologue by telling about my age. Humans are so fascinated with age.

Because human history began about six thousand years ago, many people think that my history commenced simultaneously with that of humans. No, a thousand times no. Those six centuries, give or take a few hundred years, represent human history, not mine. However, I was around when the first man was molded, shaped, fashioned, and enlivened with the ability to suck in and breathe out air. At the start of humankind, angels became "man-watchers." That was nearly six thousand years ago, and I have been watching, observing, and predicting human actions ever since.

Next to the magnificence of Creator, His shaping of humankind was the second most inter-esting phenomenon ever witnessed by angels. The procedure captured the very attention of the heav-enly hosts. Many angels virtually gazed from the portals of Heaven or hovered over the precise spot where Creator stooped to shape a tiny likeness of

Himself. All of Heaven was impressed by this "min-iature" of Creator. Gabriel announced, "Creator has made a man, a spiritual likeness of Himself!" And angels cheered. Their hoopla could be heard above the moons and suns of every planet, echoed in every black hole in the universe; the roar of the angelic applause extended throughout the galaxies.

Adam, as Creator eventually called him, was not physically strong like the angels; nonethe-less, Creator endowed him with great powers. Cre-ator gave Adam the opportunity to categorize and name all the animals, fish, and birds. Next Adam was endowed with the ability to give and receive affec-tion. He readily and genuinely accepted Creator's affection for him and returned love by way of respect, obedience, and appreciation. Best of all (or should I say worst?), Adam was a prototype who could pro-duce generations after generations of little Adams. The whole scenario involving this "new kid on the block" proved distasteful to me!

In my opinion, Adam was an insignificant creature that Creator fashioned out of burnt orange clay. He was better than the creatures he named, but lower than angels, which meant he was not as big or as strong. He was an Earth-dweller who could only exist in the natural realm and could not transport from Earth to Heaven at any given moment like we angels could. Have you seen the *Star Trek* series in which an actor may say, "Beam me up, Scottie?" Well, simi-lar to being "beamed up," angels travel in space to any destination in a relatively short time. Only we do not need the help of "Scottie" or anyone else for that matter. Angels travel faster than the speed of light, even fallen angels like me.

So why was there so much ado about this Adam, this "new addition" to Earth? What made Adam's existence so special that angels cheered? I, too, was puzzled. To me, angels are far superior to humans. What does it matter that angels cannot speak anything into existence or cannot return love? In my opinion, bigger and stronger equal better!

Nevertheless, Creator had uniquely gifted Adam. Adam did not need to be big or strong. His strength was in his spoken words, and Creator "had his back."

So everything changed in Heaven after "A-dam," as Creator called him, was molded, given breath, and actually came into existence. Adam captured the very heart of Creator.

At first, I just watched and thought, *Hmhmhmhm*. I must admit that I, too, was fascinated with the "man creature." However, more than anything else, I resented his presence on Earth.

However, Creator and the heavenly host felt differently about this unusual creation. To Creator, it was "having a child," a prototype, who would produce generation after generation, who would possess a creative spirit, a propensity to create, procreate and, re-create just like Creator Himself.

Am I repeating myself? I have a need to repeat! Creator's attention to His prototype upset me to no end. What distressed me most about the whole business of a "man" on Earth was the love that was showered upon him by Creator. Creator adored the "man creature" and openly expressed His affection!

It was at "man's" inception that I became aware that if I wanted to have any authority in the universe whatsoever, I had to take control of "man." For Creator had given the Earth to him for his possession, and that gift should have been mine!

So I have spent nearly six thousand years trying to convince humankind of his inferiority, reminding him as often as I can that he is not special. He is merely another animal in a kingdom of animals. To every human mind that is open to suggestions from "defrocked angels" like me, my hordes and I speak a language, highlighting their powerlessness and insignificance.

Why do I try to convince humans of their worthlessness? Essentially, I envy humankind. If they listen to my "sermons" and accept what I proclaim, their progress in any area of their miserable existence is halted. I provide barriers—mental, emotional, sometimes physical, but mostly social barriers. Humans may possess godlike traits, but those whom I am able to deter will never put their "godlike qualities" to use! I see to it, for I am committed to the complete frustration, failure, or annihilation of humankind.

Do you remember when I said earlier—that angels became people watchers at the inception of human existence on Earth? Well, let me elucidate further.

Just imagine this spectacle. Creator has a replica of Himself, Adam, running all over a garden for many years. Each day Adam, a so-called original scientist, is fascinated by his new discoveries. Upset to no end are words that describe me perfectly. Adam gets to name the animals, and that is too much for any fallen angel to swallow. So what do I do? I spy on Adam.

Some of Adam's early afternoons are spent walking across the river Pison, Gihon, Hiddekel, or Euphrates. He walks about on water, sits upright, or swims about as he labels the sea creatures that live in these rivers. At the end of each day, Adam sits in the presence of Creator and brags about his daily exploits. He sits with Creator face-to-face! Am I jealous or what? Nevertheless, Adam is having a good time. Creator is having a marvelous time.

The very nerve of Adam! I tell myself that either Adam is ignorant, nervy, or just plain dumb! Doesn't he know that he should stand or bow or prostrate himself in the presence of Creator? My sense of decorum is outraged! I am enraged by Adam's comfortableness in Creator's presence! And Creator allows it! So jealous am I that I want to scream!

I try to speak with Adam several times to tell him how he is expected to behave—what is accepted protocol in Creator's presence, but Adam does not allow me a chance to get a word in. Whenever I try to talk to Adam, he quotes Creator. His response would begin: *Creator says*. . . . It is literally impossible to talk to him!

Adam responds like a robot each time I try communicating, and robots would not be invented for another six thousand years! Finally, I give up! I stop trying to communicate with Adam because his conversation is always about the positive attributes of Creator. I do not care to hear about the attributes of Creator!

It is around this time that envy stirs in my heart. I first realize that Creator's devoting so much of His time to this "man-creature" is making me envious. Envy steeps inside of me long enough until that emotion becomes jealousy. Jealousy eventually mutates into hatred. I begin to loathe the human, the object of Creator's affection.

Do you understand the point that I am trying to get across? I was not created to love; I had been created to obey. Yet, I had learned to hate. Creator's display of love for Adam made me furious.

At that particular time, I felt that if Creator so valued an insignificant, inferior lump of clay over beings as powerful and as gorgeous as I, then I would show Creator how insignificant a role man would play in His Creation.

# CHAPTER II

So what am I? I am a purveyor of hate, an evil spirit. Does this revelation frighten you? Or are you doubtful that evil exists?

Have you ever sensed a vibe in a room, a house, or a town that made you extremely uncomfortable? For example, you are alone on a park bench, or standing near the edge of a lake or streambed or seated in a chair in a spacious room. Yet you feel as if you are not alone. You begin to experience a sense of eeriness. Goose bumps line your arms, and the hairs at the nape of your neck stand at attention. On the other hand, you sense you are being watched by some undefined entity. Via peripheral, you glimpse a form, a shadow, a figure. When you turn to face what you think should be another person, you see empty space instead.

Most eerie of all is getting lost in a city. You do not know your way around, yet you sense you are in an area where evil resides. For directions, you choose to stop at one gas station or restaurant after passing others because instinctively you recognize that your reception at the first group of establishments may not be as inviting as you would like. So you choose to drive on and take your chances without asking for any directions whatsoever because your "second sense" tells you that none of the nearby facilities are places where a traveler should stop to ask questions. You would prefer to get lost rather than to interact with attendants at places where you feel uncomfortable because you perceive that evil is nearby.

How do I know about this? Remember, I have observed humankind since he took his place of Earth. Consciously or unconsciously, humans are connected to the world of the spirit, an invisible world where good and evil angels abide.

Perhaps just the opposite experience may happen. For instance, you enter a city in the wee hours of the morning. You get a feeling of having inhaled fresh air, a feeling of well being. You feel as if you are totally safe; you are in a good and pleasant place. You perceive that in this town the people are friendly, so you pull off the road to eat at a nearby diner. Sure enough, everybody in the "dive"—wait-ress, waiter, even other customers—exude "auras" of friendliness. You feel as if you are in the presence of angels, good angels that is. I have heard people say this, and they are usually right. I stand back and watch the bevy of—"good angels" surrounding the place. Of course, I keep my distance! All that friend-liness is sickening to me.

Call this "sensing" whatever you will, but consider this: Perhaps in both scenarios you are in the company of angels.

Since time immemorial, or at least since my creation, two worlds have existed: one visible, the other invisible—one natural, the other supernatu-ral. My place is in one of these worlds, the invisible world, a supernatural sphere, but periodically, I try to make my way into the visible sphere. When I do so, I wreak havoc! Aha!

In the world of spirits, an invisible sphere, billions of good and evil spirit beings move about freely. Here, we are not confined by bodies.

Believe it or reject it. What do I care?

I was created. Yes, a created being, one of many angels created long before Creator formed Adam and gave Adam godlike qualities. Was I formed in the image of Creator as Adam was? No, I was spoken into existence. *And Creator said, "Let there be angels!"* And angels came into existence. No special mention about creation of angels!

So now you get it. So, what am I? An angel, a fallen angel. Or maybe you don't get it. (I sometimes wonder about humans' ability to comprehend.) Whether you understand or not, I remain a fallen angel with great aspirations!

I plan to rule the cosmos. In so doing, I want to eliminate from existing worlds all knowledge of Creator and any signs of His sovereignty. I want to prove to Him that humankind collectively is spiritually defective, and His placing them in a special place in Creation was and is a massive blunder. In so doing, I shall defame Creator as well!

I do not care about events in human history. No emotion inside of me makes me mind about anything. I know that in the very beginning Creator was, not I. He established the heavens and fashioned the

Earth, not the Earth that you presently occupy, but one that preceded this Earth as you know it, a place I refer to as the original Earth. It had everything your refurbished Earth has except for humankind. The meddlesome humans came much later.

The original Earth became formless and void as the result of a great cataclysm that took place in the universe. That upheaval was produced by a war in Heaven. A war, I am proud to say, I orchestrated. In the war, battles were fought among angels for rights to planet Earth. The armies of angels were so numerous and powerful that our fighting wreaked havoc in the universe. Planets were left desolate. Moons were splattered, and craters were formed. Suns were punctured with holes. Stars fell from their positions in space. Saturn was left with particles of comets, meteors, and stars circling the planet. Jupiter was left an icy wasteland. Earth was left dark, formless, and empty. It had to be restored.

How was I instrumental in causing the war in Heaven, which left Earth unfit for habitation by humans or angels? What happened as a result of my being "naughty"? I got the worst "beating" of all time, in human's recorded history as well as that of angel's recorded history. There is no event in human history that can compare to the defeat my army sustained. All the wars in mankind's history, those fought with sticks, swords, dynamite, or bombs—from the conflict between Cain and Abel, to every nation's civil war, to World Wars I and II—no weaponry is comparable in explosiveness to the angelic onslaught waged in Heaven.

Do I regret my actions? No. I laugh at the collections of dullards called humans who always approach a subject with their "human way of thinking." Some humans question whether I am capable of repentance. Are they stupid or what? Aha, aha. What these simpletons may never understand is that I have no capacity to repent. "Pickled" arrogance leaves no room for regrets. My arrogance has become a permanent part of my persona!

The unrepentant catalyst that provoked the war in Heaven, that's me. Overt arrogance led to my current status as a fallen angel and my expulsion from the presence of Creator. Originally, I was created an adult angel with great strength, famed good looks, and multiple talents. In Heaven, I was called Lucifer, which means "bearing light." For eons, my home was right there in Heaven. Long before man's creation, I had a great role in Heaven. Like the warring archangel, Michael, and the dutiful messenger archangel, Gabriel—I, too, was an archangel. I was the angel assigned to bring praises from Earth up to Creator. In fact, my voice was designed exclusively to sing songs of praise. My vocal chords were made perfect, far more melodious than any musical instrument ever made, fashioned, or formed. Even today, whatever the pitch, my voice can reach it; whatever the song, I can sing it. Not only can I sing in all octaves, but I can also imitate the sound of every musical instrument. I was simultaneously Heaven's choir director and orchestra leader. In today's vernacular, I was a one-angel band.

What were my duties in Heaven? I waited on Creator. I was His angelic valet. At first, as Creator's awesome power and penetrating radiance shone on me, I was in awe as I served Him. I was innocent and contented to serve, and I experienced honor in my servitude. For eons I "watched Creator's back," which needs no watching.

So why was I His servant? It was my job. Originally, I was mesmerized by Creator's powerful presence and was engulfed by His powerful aura. Was I under a spell! Sometimes I roamed the majestic mountains of Heaven where I had time to think, or I spiraled down to Earth where I really had time to ponder the fate of the universe. I often stood at the entrance of Creator's temple where I observed His regalia—His regalness, elegance, jeweled garments, lofty temple. He was worshipped day and night. The elegance, power, and worship made me jealous. My reactions were similar to those of infamous Judas who carried Joshua's moneybags and eventually betrayed his benefactor for thirty pieces of silver. How much of another's wealth can one manage before he wants it for his own? How much of another's power can one observe before he wants it for himself? I decided I should have it all—wealth, power, and worship!

I am sure most humans can understand a valet wanting to run the manor. Well, my desire to be in charge was similar. The progression of my rebellion started gradually. First, I commenced feeling important because of my rank in Heaven, which allowed me to absorb light from Creator and exposed me to His ultimate wealth. His presence radiated such power. Why couldn't some of that glorious energy radiate from me, and not from Creator alone?

Narcissism, you say. Yes! A million times yes! I began to consider myself a class act. Vanity (what an appropriate word!) led to my craving a "piece of the universal pie," and eventually wanting it all!

As I moved about Heaven performing my angelic duties, deep inside my intellect, rebellious thoughts emerged and took root. First, I began believing and behaving as if I were better than the average angel. As I pondered my superiority over the angels, eventually I began to compare myself to Creator. Finally, I concluded that perhaps I, too, could be as great as Creator. However, I knew from experience that there could be only one "boss." My decision to challenge Creator's sovereignty made me a rebel. I had plans to run the universe.

Initially, I just perceived that things could be different. Nothing is wrong with that way of thinking, right? It was not my fault that I was surrounded by magnificent wealth, given great beauty and talent, made superior to man and angels. If I blame anybody for the circumstances I now find myself in, I blame Creator! Why give me abilities and not let me do things my own way?

Do you know something? Creator knew what I was up to from the very moment my heart changed towards Him. Yet He never tried to stop me! Like humans, I blame Him for any and all predicaments in which I find myself. Why should I not blame Him?

To continue, my becoming rebellious did not occur overnight. Actually, it took thousands and thousands of years. At first, I merely commented on Creator's judgments. Next I questioned the veracity of whatever He commanded. Finally, I openly criticized Creator's ability to manage situations surrounding Heaven and the Earth.

In Heaven, I began to voice my opinions about how earthly affairs were managed. To any angel that cared to listen, I began to make subtle suggestions of a possible "take-over," similar to what Absalom did to his father David; only my supposed subtlety was on a grander scale. Initially, every angel rejected my suppositions and shunned my presence, but I persisted. Each day after I completed my duties, I got up on my "soapbox." Cunningly, I maligned the name, capability, and words of Creator. Eventually, one or two angels humored me by listening to what I had to say. Although angels are created beings and are free to choose whom they will serve, I never expected a single angel to choose me instead of Creator. I was surprised when a bevy of angels showed up on the west side of Heaven, far away from the throne room, to hear me speak my thoughts. (You don't think I had the courage to do this in front of the throne, do you?)

After much persuasion, I finally formed a conspiracy among angels that were vulnerable to my "charm." First, it was only opinions that gave way to overt criticism. Criticisms lead to debates that eventually convinced some of the angelic audience that my assessment of Creator's management style might be worth considering. My malicious opinions and lengthy negative speeches corrupted me, and the angels that listened to me and were convinced by my continuously complaining about how Creator should or should not do things, likewise became corrupted. They were now my posse, my crew, my gang, whatever you prefer to call them. I became their leader, and they paid homage to me. Exactly what I wanted, worship. The word "corruption" was invented to describe me. Am I special or what?

The horde from the west side of Heaven was in agreement with me that I, Lucifer, could rule Heaven better than Creator. So once I had a backing, I felt that I could successfully take Creator's place and rule Heaven and subsequently Earth. What would I do with Creator? I felt He should retire!

What an orator I had become! Wow! I was able to rally 33 percent of Heaven's angels. I was now in a position where I could vie to usurp the very authority of Creator! I strutted around Heaven like a peacock with its feathers spread. Was I ever surprised at the results of my bid for supremacy!

My attempt to take over Heaven caused a war in Heaven that was most fierce. The battle was among angels, the strongest immortal warriors in the universe. Neither side could die, so it was a war of strength between loyal and disloyal angels. The blows were lightning fast and thunderous upon impact. The cosmic elements—suns, moons, stars, planets—all were affected. The brightness of the sun was impeded by multitudes of battling angels. Voluminous and threatening cumulus clouds plastered the skies. Torrents of rain poured continuously because the force of nature was disrupted by the conflict in the spirit world. As millions of angelic swords clashed in the heavens in a battle for angelic domination, bolt after bolt of lightning flashed; the thunder rolled and roared. Electrical energy emitted from clashing angelic swords sent lightning bolts throughout the skies and down to Earth. Lightning bolts struck trees, so entire forests burned to the ground. Day and night were the same, pure darkness. In the spirit world, multitudes of huge magnificent angels with flaming swords thrust and heaved back and forth; striking victims that momentarily faltered then regrouped and struck the same targets again and again. Angels were severed in half, dematerialized, and then materialized again. There seemed to be no end to the war.

Then something dramatic happened. Michael, the archangel, stepped out on a cloud in plain view, and abruptly, the fighting halted. On both sides, angels loyal to Creator and angels loyal to me, Lucifer, stood at attention in midair with swords frozen in their hands. Thousands times ten thousand of angels watched in stillness, yet poised and ready to do battle. All eyes were on Michael.

At Michael's appearance, the angelic battle was suspended, and both sides of the warring angelic opponents, the good and the rebellious, showed respect for Creator's captain.

A solemn hush settled over angelic warriors. In time, which mimicked slowed motion, the loyal angels smiled as they saluted their champion.

Welcome or unwelcome, Michael stood alone in the middle of the air above all other angels. His right hand clutched a flaming golden sword, the length of which was more than half of Michael's height of thirteen or more feet. The tip of the gigantic sword pointed earthward. With his left hand raised, Michael's fingers beckoned to me to come and fight with him.

"Satan, come and do battle!" his voiced thundered. I hesitated briefly at the sound of the new nomenclature. Never before had I been called Satan. The name became me, and I became the name. (It has a little ring to it; don't you think?)

Because of Michael's challenge, the battle could then be fought with an end in sight. The struggle would be between the archangel, Michael, and the dark angel, Satan, as I would be called throughout human history. The war was now a battle of archangels, the righteous obedient Michael against the rebellious Lucifer who had become Satan. The victor would determine the winning side.

I had strength. I had power. I had beauty! What else was necessary to overpower Michael? So what if he was dazzling brightly and massively built?

I charged faster than the speed of light and

with a force greater than pressure needed to split an atom. The wide expanse of Michael's chest was my intended "bull's eye." Within seconds of my calculated impact with this burly angelic form, Michael merely stepped aside. I missed him completely! Instead, I landed on Earth's sun. Because of the forceful plunge I had exerted in my assault, my landing formed craters on the sun. Michael merely turned in my direction and waited. Filled with pride, I immediately regrouped and resumed my attack. I missed him again! I did an about-face and continued to charge his form, but each onslaught was useless. Each time I charged the archangel, he merely shifted his position within seconds of my sword making contact, and I found myself slashing at empty space. When I turned to make what was to be my final assault, I felt a tremendous blow across my upper torso. Michael's sword had made contact with my angelic form. For an instant, the thunderous blow knocked most of the wind out of me. Yet I managed to stay in the fray. We fought, bright angel against dark angel, great strength against greater strength.

Immediately I recognized that Michael's strength was far greater than my own! I also realized that he was a master at fighting. Various thoughts ran through my mind. *If Creator knows all things*, I thought, *surely He must have known that this battle would come to pass. If He knew about the battle, He must have known what I was up to all the time. If He knew, why did He allow this to happen? Why would He allow me to suffer utter humiliation? He could have put a stop to all of this before any of it started. Why didn't He do something?* I blamed Creator for the predicament in which I found myself.

As I rapidly pondered my imminent defeat, Michael's powerful sword slashed across my head, my chest, and my back. I was about to feign surrender, but his massive left hand, like giant pliers, caught hold of my throat and tightened. I was powerless in the clutches of the mightiest of angels. I was shaken as the Earth is shaken with the force of an earthquake. Like a rag doll in the mouth of leviathan, I was battered up and down, back and forth. The hordes of angels that had joined me in mutiny stood silently in awe as they witnessed Michael's angelic strength, which neither they nor I could match. Like a listless dead serpent bound for a rubbish heap, I lay helpless in the powerful grip of Michael, Creator's holy archangel. The hordes of mutinous angels shrank and cowered at his awesome strength. No other disloyal angel dared challenge the towering monument of power. I had no back up. That day I vowed to never again challenge Michael.

As I realized that my bid to take over Heaven had failed miserably, Michael lifted my angelic form above his head, wielded it in a circle faster and mightier than the force of seven tornadoes, and hurled me downward. I was thrown out of Heaven by a mere angel! On the way down, I collided with several planets, their moons and stars.

I landed in Earth's stratosphere. As I sat in space and pondered my predicament, I watched as angel after angel was also thrown down to Earth. They were the ones that had joined me in my failed take over. Some angels fell directly at my feet; others fell nearby. Along with me, one third of Heaven's angels had become fallen angels, to never again live in the presence of Creator. Before the war, I had great beauty. After I was kicked out of Heaven, my magnificent beauty vanished. Likewise, my mutinous cohorts lost their beauty as well. We no longer reflected light. We had lost our permanent residency in Heaven. So what?

After all the commotion in the universe subsided, Adam, a clueless twit, gets to set up shop on a refurbished Earth where he is allowed to roam about safely. He is given a deed to a garden, east of Eden.

# CHAPTER III

Okay. Perhaps you now understand what I was and what I have become.

By trying to rise to the throne of Creator, I caused mutiny in Heaven, which led to an angelic war. Michael, Creator's "seven star" general, along with loyal angels, won the battle, and I was thrown out of Heaven. One third of the angels, those that had joined me in our failed "take over," were thrown out of Heaven as well. We found ourselves disconnected from the sustaining light of Creator and forever damned. What do I mean when I say *damned*? I mean forever disconnected from the mindset of Creator. I mean to be consciously aware of His attributes and all the possibilities connected with serving Him, but never to live in His magnificent presence or experience oneness with Him. To be forever separated from Creator for all eternity is to be damned. And that is my position today.

My future is even bleaker. Very soon I shall be eternally punished for the harm I currently inflict on humankind. I shall be judged and punished for hurting humankind whom Creator adores. So in the meantime, I shall do my utmost to inflict all the harm that is demonically possible on Creator's simple-minded twits called humans. This I do especially well.

So who am I? If you were to use the words *satan* or *devil* to define my character, most people would just laugh and say, *I really don't believe in a devil. There is no such thing! The devil is merely a figment of man's imagination.*

Others might question your intellect. *Surely,* they might say, *only the ignorant and uneducated believe in beings like demons and devils.* However, most people believe in angels, don't they? Okay. One of many fallen angels, that's me. Of this group, I rank as the most powerful, so I do my "own thing." That is, I have started my own kingdom. Although my realm is of darkness and despair, I get a chance to run it just the same, for I deal with the darker side of life.

Adam's authority on the Earth convinced me that I might have a shot at being a leader of something. Any planet in the solar system would have been okay, except these were minus one element. They could not sustain life, and I prefer to rule living, breathing beings, not just a band of disgruntled fallen angels.

Nevertheless, just look what happened next! Creator assigned Earth as a place for man's enjoyment, not just a place to work and live. What sense did it make to give to this "man creature" a prize as valuable as Earth? He was clueless about what to do with a planet as gorgeous as Earth! I, on the other hand, could think of millions of things to do on Earth. When Creator gave Adam the deed to Earth, I decided to make a "puppet" of Creator's "man creature." I would steal the Earth from Adam! Creator had not annihilated me from existence. Perhaps I still had a chance to rule something! I had had no success at takeover thus far.

Make no mistake about it. In the past, I wanted to rule the Earth, and today I still want to rule this planet. Why shouldn't I be allowed to rule here? I was once given the task of serving in the presence of Creator. If I could serve in Heaven, why shouldn't I be capable of running a planet? Earth is ideal.

So in order to outsmart Adam, I had to learn and understand his nature, but first I had to overcome my limitations. Contrary to popular opinion, I am unipresent, which means I can only be in one place at a time, so I had to deploy multiple bands of fallen angels to spy on Adam and keep me apprised of his activities. Even my surveillance was limited. For whenever Creator made daily visits to the garden to talk with Adam, all spying activities were shut down. Moreover, I do not know everything. I had to learn about Adam just as he had to learn about his environment. If I appear smart, it is because I am lucky to have been schooled in the universe longer than man has existed, and I have had access to all of mankind's philosophies, histories, sciences, languages, music, beliefs, customs, traditions, and superstitions. Moreover, I am a keen observer of humans.

I learned early in mankind's history that Adam need only obey Creator, and Adam would live forever. Can you imagine my looking at Adam's face for all eternity? I had to come up with a plan to destroy Adam!

Adam's presence and ownership of Earth became a sore spot with me, a "bone of contention." He was "too good to be true," if you know what I mean. I had to rid the world of him. After having escaped extinction at just a word from Creator and by the hands of Michael, I learned of the experience called *death*. There could be an end to life, an experience not familiar to angels. I concentrated my newfound knowledge on finding ways to bring about Adam's death.

There had to be a breakdown of some kind to start an elimination process, a dying process. I could not "stomach" Adam for the rest of eternity! Do you want to know something? It would take over 900 years for Adam to die!

I was looking for a way to rid the Earth of Adam when I got some extraordinary news. It was noised about Heaven that Creator wanted Adam to have a mate, one made especially for Adam. All of the animals, sea creatures, and birds had mates. It was only fair that Adam should be with his own kind. So Creator, using the marrow from one of Adam's ribs, fashioned a man with a womb, which He called "woman" to be Adam's mate.

He placed Adam in a deep sleep, removed a bone and flesh from his side, and sculptured a raving beauty as a mate for Adam. For her to be part of Adam as Creator had envisioned, Creator used Adam's bone and flesh to make her uniquely Adam's.

Adam's handsomeness was a sight to behold, but the beauty of the woman took away the breath of angels. Angels loyal to Creator praised the work of the Creator. We who were dislodged from Heaven just watched in awe.

Curiously, I observed. I could not help comparing the woman's beauty to the good looks I had lost. I had been made the most beautiful of angels, but this woman's beauty rivaled the very beauty I once possessed. The woman was gorgeous!

The consummation of their union was unlike anything angels had ever witnessed! Wow! The touching, the caressing—the sheer ecstasy was so wholesome, so pleasurable, so exciting that angels watched in amazement. Angels loyal to Creator were excited and applauded Creator for His ingenuity because He gave to humankind the capacity to mate whereby they gave joy and pleasure to each other. Intercourse between the man and woman encompassed their entire being, body, soul, and spirit. Creator established the act. No such ecstasy was exhibited among animals and birds while mating; their coming together was to perform a vital function, to procreate. Among angels, sexual intercourse was unheard of. The sex act between the man and woman appeared to make each seem complete. The man completed the woman, and she completed him. The accolades of the angels in Heaven could be heard all the way down on Earth. They praised Creator's inventiveness in forming beings that have capacities to express love to each other.

Subsequently, I felt cheated. Why should these "upstarts" experience sexual pleasures that angels were denied? I was so stirred with jealousy that I determined to observe, examine, and distort the use of sex if I could. So I spent much of my time examining and learning about this new thing called *intimacy*.

When in Heaven, I experienced a certain intimacy with Creator, for I was called the "anointed cherub that covered." The pleasure and ecstasy in serving and obeying Creator and merely being in His presence was joy in itself. It was the type of joy that brought about contentment. My arrogance and poor judgment robbed me of the fulfilling joy that I had attained when I was an archangel in Heaven. After being kicked out of Heaven, I became the epitome of emptiness, cruelty, and hate. So naturally, I envied the man and the woman their newfound intimacy. If given a chance, I would steal it from them!

Since they were the "only game in town," I looked for every opportunity to rob them of their peacefulness. I followed the pair. Of course, neither the woman nor Adam could see me, for I exist in the spirit world, and they were in the natural realm. Yet they knew when I was nearby. They sensed it!

Meanwhile, I was fascinated by the woman's beauty, and at the same time, I hated her for it. I hated Adam even more, for Creator had made the woman uniquely special for Adam's enjoyment alone. Adam could realize happiness, joy, contentment—the emotions that I no longer experienced and would never experience again. At that point in time, I vied for control of Adam and the woman!

Every step they made, I followed—except, of course, when Creator visited them in the cool of the afternoons. That was the time of day when Creator and Adam talked, and I had enough sense to stay away. (I may be many things, but I am not stupid.)

Would you believe that the great Creator actually spent many of His afternoons visiting and talking with this pair? Believe it. He did.

The beauty of the woman Creator had sculpted for Adam and the sexual act between them fascinated angels. The angels of God were impressed at the successful work of Creator, but for us angels who had been thrown out of Heaven, it became a nightmare. We were jealous! It was at this time that fallen angels yearned to test their impish and evil behaviors. And whom did they want to test these on? You guessed it! Humans! Many fallen angels became obsessed with the sexual act. Thousands desired to have relations with the man, and an even greater number of fallen angels desired to have intercourse with the woman. So many of us became obsessed with thoughts of mating in general, and we pondered day and night *what if's*. What if each of the humans would mate with a non-human? Possibly with a fallen angel? In our fallen state, we became so obsessed with human sexuality; our obsession drove us deeper into depravity. There were no sexual acts that skipped our imaginations.

So Adam and the woman's existence triggered a host of fallen angels to descend further and further into an abyss of lewdness and lasciviousness.

All of the deviant and perverted sexual acts that only our intellects could invent, we fallen angels wanted to see humans perform. We, the evil hordes, desired to participate in or perform sexual acts on humans. Within the imaginations of fallen angels, ideas of deviant sexual behaviors came into existence in the spirit world and eventually made its way into the natural realm.

For greater understanding of things, let us ret-rogress a bit. I lead million of fallen angels. However, my leadership over this horde did not come about by an election as you might presume. I have power over them because I was made mentally, physically, and emotionally stronger than all of the fallen angels. Second, I am intellectually the most devious of them all. My strength and intelligence have nothing to do with me. Creator made me stronger and more power-ful than this "crew" that I now manage because of the role for which I was originally created. I was created to serve as number three in power among the angels in Heaven. It was not Creator's intent that I should lead a horde of rebellious rejects from Heaven. That choice was mine.

I hate the hordes that I command almost as much as I hate humans, for I am a purveyor of hate. However, there are no words in any language to describe the depth of my hatred for humans! Abhor, detest, revile—all these words do not express the volume of my loathing for humankind. (Yet some actually think I care! Is this laughable or what?)

Because I want to rule something, I now

command the most despicable, depraved, ghastly evil group in the universe. I rule them because I am the most contemptible, corrupt, and evil of the entire bunch.

Now that I have made myself clear, let me resume my monologue.

It was my presence in the garden that caused me to earn the names, tempter, serpent, and devil. You are aware of which nomenclature I go by most, aren't you? You guessed it. Devil. To me, the word "devil" has more impish appeal. Plus the word scares humans.

So let me tell you how I went after the woman who was made for Adam.

# CHAPTER IV

I hate. I hate babies and little children. I hate their parents and grandparents, their friends, neighbors, their teachers—everyone! I even hate animals!

Does my admission of hatred for Creation disgust you? Why should it? Am I human that I should care about babies or about anyone for that matter? I am not human, and I am incapable of caring. At times, I levitate, dumbfounded by the reasoning of humans. Many have this "semi-pristine" view of me. They expect me to carry out attacks on adults, but never on children. How stupid humans are! Sometimes I rate humankind's ability to reason and arrive at conclusions lower than that of the dumbest of animals.

What do you think drives child molesters to victimize children? Or pedophiles to solicit, abduct, rape, or murder "wee" ones? These are driven to do as they do. I claim the infamous title of "Director of Evil." So why would you think that my evil practices would exclude innocents such as babies? My mission is to steal, kill, and destroy. No human is excluded.

I post evil sentries at parks, schools, playgrounds, and even at churches and orphanages. These fallen angels or demons coach potential stalkers, peeping toms, kidnappers, rapists, and killers. Repulsive demonic spirits spy on little boys and girls who are vulnerable and alone. Vicious demons persuade vacuous humans with pliable psyches to stalk, kidnap, rape, or kill children, even the tiniest babies. Once we evil spirits have child molesters and the likes under our control, these deviants do to children exactly what demons desire to do to children, fondle, molest, or kill—starve, strangle, or maim.

I abhor all humans, but I detest children most! If humans did not have children, then the race of humankind would have ceased to exist long ago! I blame children for the continuation of the human race!

Moreover, I hate the elderly. A bunch of useless cripples pretending to have dignity and wisdom. A universal waste of time. I employ vicious demons of cruelty to drive a social wedge between the elderly and their children or families or caregivers. I am especially partial to their abuse. My hordes from hell are forever trying to frustrate the minds of caregivers to cause harm or mistreatment of the doting, bed-wetting, weather-beaten burdens on society. I do my best to convince any human who will listen that the elderly are useless and should be put out of their uselessness. I have had a measure of success, but I shall not rest until disposal of the elderly becomes international law.

I hate the poor and the physically and mentally challenged. I assigned demonic spirits to stir up malice and discontent at welfare centers, housing projects, handicap centers, and nursing homes. I even post evil spirits in many unlikely places such as doctors' offices, restaurants, shopping malls, and grocery stores. I want to destroy the hardy, but the downtrodden I especially want to destroy. I revile humans in general; the innocent, sick, or helpless I hate most of all!

I preside at massacres, murders, rapes, human sacrifices, and cannibalistic rituals. Yes, I, Satan, hate you! I, the very one that some humans have chosen to consider as friend, hate every mortal or immortal in the universe! I even hate Creator! Eve trusted me, and it cost her dearly.

Can you imagine what it was like when the very first woman was targeted by oppressive spirits? You cannot imagine. Your imagination cannot stretch that far. Today in my bid to deceive, I have to divide demons, evil spirits, strong men, and imps among hundreds of thousands of "do-gooders." So my hordes are spread rather thin. However, in my onslaught on Eve, every fallen angel, at one time or other, took part in that assignment.

Why was she the subject of a devilish onslaught? She was told by Adam not to touch a certain tree. I merely wanted her to thwart Adam's command. Hence, she would also indirectly disobey Creator, since Adam had received the mandate and not her.

Undisciplined, evil, and ornery fallen angels used seduction on this our training mission. Yes, it was in the Garden, east of Eden, where fallen angels first experimented on oppressing humans. Outright possession was not an option as it is in modern times, for demons had not yet evolved.

How do evil spirits oppress a subject? By transmitting tormenting thoughts that result in mental unrest. We gauge the depth of concentration depending upon the victim's susceptibility to the spirit world. Some people are more predisposed than others are. In the case of Eve, she was innocent, innocent, innocent! The contingent of fallen angels assigned to alter Eve's way of thinking, to reject Adam's directive evoked sheer torment inside of Eve's intellect. The torment spilled over into her spirit and affected her emotionally.

How did I figure out what was happening inside of Eve's spirit? Eve said so. I have had years to observe the species, to learn and decipher emotional and spiritual codes. However, there is no real mystery in deciphering emotions of most humans. I need only listen to what they have to say to learn what is happening inside of them.

What are our tactics? Because of our invisibility, a contingent of evil spirits first invades a victim's space. That is, we crowd, encircle, and occupy the very same space our victim occupies. Our target may sense our presence but cannot prove that we are there. Next, my hordes and I repeat words the victim has said, or we suggest an outcome of which we imagine our prey might be scared. Evil spirits repeatedly yell and scream the actions we want our victim to act out. Sometimes, a psychic connection takes place; that is, we convince the human to do as we suggest. When it happens, we cheer because we know that we have made contact with the prey, and he or she might do as we suggest. It worked first on Eve. Once I discovered this strategy for oppressing humans, I stuck with it. Repetitive psychic hounding has been most effective thus far!

Boring, you say? Yes, boring, but effective! Whoever claimed that demons and evil spirits are creative in the first place? Are humans so dimwitted that they do not know evil spirits cannot devise original schemes? Usually, humans help us set traps. Humans express; evil spirits react. Evil spirits act on what we hear humans say and what we see humans do. We just build the traps that humans express; we zero in on what humans fear.

What did you think? Did you actually think that evil spirits can read your mind? Come on! Are humans so dense that they do not know that evil spirits cannot read minds?

In the garden, million of evil spirits, with no one else to harass, concentrated all their manipulative skills and power on Eve. In her space, invisible evil forces swerved in and out, zoomed round and about her, some whispering, others shouting at her. The very aura of malevolent spirits, the electricity emitted in the evil airwaves, her senses—all resounded with the presence of unseen satanic activities as we practiced our theory of seduction. How unfortunate for the woman. She had no clue as to what was happening round and about her in the spirit world. Millions and millions of fallen angels shouting, chanting, *Eve,*

*the tree! Look at the tree. My, isn't it a delight to see?*
*Touch the tree, Eve. Eve, touch the tree!*

When I go after victims today, it is far different from when we attacked our first victim, Eve, as the woman became known. Today when I assign spirits to torment victims, I have to divvy up my satanic horde because there are millions and millions targeted for destruction, and angels, fallen or otherwise, can only be in one place at a time.

In Eve's case, she expressed that she felt as if stone upon stones were piled high upon her head, and she carried the weight around day and night, night and day.

I remember the first day I went after her. That morning she had been complaining to Adam that he did not spend enough time with her during the day. You should have heard her whine.

*Why, Adam, you spend all morning overlooking the Garden and its operations. In the afternoons, Creator shows up, and you give Him all of your attention. I am by myself most of the time. I get tired of talking to animals! I need human company. After all,* she continues, *you are the only other human.*

Unknown to her, I stalked her in the spirit realm. I wanted to talk to her face-to-face, just like Creator talked to Adam, but I had no physical form that belonged to me. I have the ability to materialize, but I must have a willing host, a live body that I can use. My only choice then was to use the frame of an animal. I approached the horse, but it shied away. The birds of the air flew away at the mere suggestion of my using their frames. Who cares? Their puniness would not have been impressive in the first place. The lions, tigers, rhinoceros, and other larger animals wanted nothing to do with me. Even the donkey refused me entry! All the animals on the face of the Earth ran from my presence except the amphibians. An untamable serpent did not object, but instead proved willing. It walked upright and talked. Its vocal instruments were so designed that it could utter speech, the very words that I wished to say. Its presence would not repel the woman, for she was accustomed to dealing with the animals, including the snakes. It was a cobra I convinced to lend me its form and voice so I could communicate with the woman.

*I see you're looking at that tree again*, I said by way of introduction.

The *fruit looks very tasty*. Deceptively charming, I made suggestions.

She did not take my "bait" on the first day or the next. As a matter of vexation, Eve did not even consider the tree or its fruit desirable for quite sometime. I, in the serpent, pretended friendship, and as my deception blossomed, so did Eve's acceptance of everything I said through the serpent. When the trap was set, that is, when she was at ease with the creature, I struck!

*Look,* I said boldly. *Has Creator said that you cannot eat of all the trees of the garden?*

She was unsuspecting and answered that Adam and she could eat of the fruit of the trees of the garden, but were not allowed to eat of the tree in the middle of the garden. She said that they would die should they eat of it, or even touch it.

*What does it mean to die?* I asked. My asking this question was sheer genius! Neither the woman nor I understood the concept of death. I knew I had been created to live forever. I took for granted that the woman and man had been made likewise. Nothing had ever died.

My education commenced in the Garden of Eden. Before then, I had knowledge, but of the angelic kind—that is, on a "need-to-know" basis. Knowledge I needed to perform in Heaven was insufficient knowledge to steal ownership of Earth from humankind. Hence, I had to obtain new information, and I had to learn from humankind. So I learned to fine-tune my reptilian skills as I watched and learned from humans.

I am purpose driven. How do I extract evil out of the good? How do I alter righteous to become unrighteous? How do I corrupt the just? I use any method of trickery that is available and any person who is agreeable.

So much drama over one tree! As Eve was then, modern day humans are still hung up on speculations about the tree of knowledge of good and evil. Let me tell you this. Ninety percent of the trees were available as food to the couple, and one was set aside for Creator. It was a tithe, but I convinced Eve to covet its fruit. Her covetousness was her first step toward sin, and I was right there cheering her on, if you can call what I do "cheering." Eve had one profound quality that I relished. She wanted what belonged to Creator, and so did I!

There was no point in trying to tempt Adam to disobey Creator. Adam—what a boor! Creator instructed Adam not to touch the tree. Adam listened. Eve questioned. Face it. Adam was just not my type. Too obedient, if you know what I mean. On the other hand, Eve had potential. Yet it took years to get her attention!

I had been kicked out of Heaven. I wanted the two humans kicked out of the garden. Why should they have such a beautiful existence while I walked up and down over the Earth? The woman made a perfect victim.

Yes, the garden was my classroom. It was there where I began learning about the weaknesses in humankind, the differences between the man and the woman. There I first discovered how to trap and snare victims into doing my bidding and how to assault them with guilt afterwards. I also learned a valuable lesson about the limitations of fallen angels. Yet the greatest of all lessons was discovering the clout attached to food, ego, and power. If I want to ensnare and corrupt, I whet a human's appetite for food, stroke his ego, and offer him a way to obtain power.

I had cornered Eve, a victim, in whose mind I transmitted an obsession to taste a mere fruit simply because she was told not to. After agreeing with Eve that she was being deprived of making choices, she and I became friendly, and finally she considered me, a serpent, a friend. Now I could speak to her face-to-face, as Creator spoke with Adam.

*Have you seen such luscious succulent look-ing fruit elsewhere in the Garden? Did Creator say that you should not touch that tree? Why not? How can the fruit of such a beautiful tree be harmful?*

I listened to her when she pleaded with Adam to spend some of his days with her, for she no longer wanted to be alone with the voice of temptation. She openly discussed her fixations and preoccupation at the mere sight of the one tree she was forbidden to touch. She said that the only time she could put the tree out of her mind was when Adam was nearby. Adam encouraged her to *"just say no"* to her obses-sion. *Talk with the animals*, he encouraged her. *They are good company when I am away*. Let's face it. Adam did not understand Eve's temptation, for he was not the one being targeted. When I overheard her speak what was in her heart, I knew I was mak-ing headway.

My experiment on how to make spiritual contact with Eve did not take a day or a month or a year. The procedure was long and arduous. First, I spent hours, days, months, years whispering to her to simply look at the beautiful tree with the untouchable fruit. I questioned her. *Who said? What did He say? Why did He say so? When did He say it? Where are you forbidden to go?*

When I had her full attention, I prompted her to desire food even though she was not hungry.

I whispered continuously, *What if all the other trees were empty of fruit? What would you eat then?*

I knew exactly when Eve decided to test the edibility of the fruit that the forbidden tree produced. She talked of its shape, size, and color and compared the fruit to others she had eaten. Eventually she took courage, with my insistence of course, to caress the fine-looking luscious green leaves on the branches of the tree. Finally, she progressed to stroking the fruit. Not long after that, the woman became bold enough to pick one, taste it, like it, and after not falling dead on the spot, sat and ate to her heart's content. To the batch of regular fruit Eve had picked for Adam's supper, she added a sample of the forbidden fruit she had enjoyed. When she did that, I knew I was about to score big!

My experiment with the human intellect was taking shape! I had learned after years of trial and error just how to infiltrate the human psyche! I now understood just a small portion of how to penetrate the intellect of a human, just enough to serve my ends. My devilish suggestions reached Eve because her mind was open and pliable—may I say idle?

The day she touched the fruit was the day I realized that my experiment on the human thinking was a success. Well, for those of you who do not know the rest of the story, I'll make it brief.

Eve ate and was satisfied. She offered the fruit to Adam, who ate and was filled. After he swallowed, she told him what he had eaten. Immediately, their lives changed. They were no longer innocent;

together they had disobeyed Creator! The process of dying had commenced! It had taken me hundreds of human years to bring about her downfall. You will never understand the satanic frustration I underwent while deceiving this pair!

There was dancing in the realm of fallen angels. I alone had foiled Creator's plan. Now the Earth would belong to me, for surely I owned these humans, or so I thought. When Creator visited on the very day of their disobedience, I learned differently.

I decided to show up in my disguise as a serpent to get the inside stuff first hand. Actually, I wanted to gloat incognito. Gloating compliments my many personalities. (Oh, didn't I tell you? I have more than one.)

When Creator's thunderous voice called for Adam, I began to shake.

"Adam!" He called so commandingly, so forcefully that I literally jumped out of the snake's skin. Because I no longer dwelled in Creator's presence, I had let it slip just how powerful His voice was. At the sound of Him, I knew that I had made a very bad decision to show up in the form of a serpent, and it was expedient that I get out of it pronto.

The next scene was a matter of who could best hide from Creator. Adam and his mate hid, for they experienced shame and guilt. I hid for two reasons. First, I was afraid of being punished for my role in the couple's deception. Next, I wanted to watch unobserved what would happen to the errant couple. (Did I say unobserved?) When the couple finally showed themselves, Adam blamed Eve; she blamed the snake; the snake blamed me. When she laid blame on the serpent, I realized then that if I had remained within the frame of the serpent just an instant longer, I might suffer dire consequences. One word from Creator, and I would be relegated to remain in the form of the snake until its death.

The pair was banished from the Garden and so was I. They were told their future, and so was I. In their future, a man like Adam would buy back his garden and restore humankind to a place of innocence and oneness with Creator. I would be damned.

By the way, the slithering creepy serpent lost its power to speak, never to communicate with humans again! Should I feel sorry for the clammy slithering dust eater? Well, it merely paid for lending me its body. I hate Earth's creatures second in intensity to which I despise humankind!

As the sadden couple left the garden hand in hand, I could not help but think, *Wow! It's a smart move I made when I exited the body of the serpent. Had I not done so before their encounter with Creator, I might have been stuck in that hideous form! Ugh!*

Well, if you want to know the rest of the story, Creator assigned huge warring angelic beings to guard the entrance to the garden. It is still guarded today. The angels hold flaming swords and keep out humans and spirits like me. Whenever I pass by during my missions to steal from, to kill, or to destroy humans, I see those no-nonsense "bouncers" on their posts. I will stay clear of that place as long as they are there. I have had my taste of defeat by the hands of Michael. Those angels look equally as threatening. Even if they are not, they can call for Michael at anytime. I don't have to hear "Step away from the garden" twice. I stay away.

The garden is no longer visible to humans since Adam and Eve's departure. Humans cannot see it with their naked eyes because it has become part of the spirit realm. They are unable to see into the world of the spirit, so they cannot see the ever-vigilant sentries. One of my personal objectives is to make sure that garden remains invisible to humankind! Humans do not deserve a place like that. They have no idea what to do with it.

Today when I pass the Garden of Eden just to check to see what's going on, I see angels with drawn swords still standing at the entrance. Their faces change from time to time, but not the swords in their hands or the threat that they wield.

# CHAPTER V

Sin? Oh, how I promote the actions associated with this word! Yet I lodged a complaint against the errant pair of humans. The "twits" disobeyed Creator; still He provided a way to cover their disobedience. Something called a blood sacrifice. He did not cover me! Instead, I get booted out of Heaven! In the meantime, these creatures, Adam and Eve, were taught how to atone for their indiscretions! Plus, they could pass down the process of sacrificing to their sons so they, too, could atone for their sins.

I could not abide the situation one moment longer, for I began to envision Creator's real plan! Why, I could visualize billions of humans, as numerous as the angels, all being forgiven for their indiscretions. Creator would still be in charge of things, and all my training and expended efforts to corrupt humankind would be for naught! No! No! No! A thousand no's! What a blow to my ego! What a blow to my kingdom!

I had to work fast. The pair did not as yet understand death, but they had experienced eviction from a garden and life was tough. I heard them say, *"If death is worse than being evicted from the garden, then we should do everything in our power to delay that experience."* I had to learn about death fast because I decided I wanted them dead!

A blood sacrifice? What is a blood sacrifice? Why is blood so important? The whole matter involving blood puzzled me. I had to learn what made blood important to Creator.

Sometimes I tracked Adam and the woman. Fallen angels after fallen angels were assigned to keep me posted of their actions. I made it hard for them to find food; I made it difficult for them to get along. And what did they do? They came together "lovingly" and had little Adams and Eves! Little humans!

When I witnessed the whole episode of the mating, the swelling of the woman's belly, I knew that Creator had pulled a "fast one" on me. He had given them the power to reproduce themselves! What was I to do? I felt for sure that at the demise of the pair, Creation would go back to business as usual. No humans, just Creator and angels. I could control the Earth, and Creator might allow me to do so, since I had so cunningly swiped it out of the hands of His errant pair! I tried to infiltrate Eve's mind regarding the risk of having a child. Birth and the process associated with birthing were foreign to her. *"But, did not Creator say . . . ?"* was her reply. Now she was quoting the words of Creator to me! Imagine that.

She saw animals give birth and was convinced that Adam and she could do even better. Foiled again. I wasn't the only one being educated. Apparently, the couple was learning from their environment too!

Would Creator let me have Earth? No! No! No! Here it was! The humans were now having babies! What was I to do? I had to rid Earth of the humans! So I devised a plan. Oh, this plot would not take hundreds of years to carry out like my experiment with Eve and the tree, for by that time, I had perfected my scheme. I had fine-tuned the food angle, and I had learned an even more powerful tool called selfishness, *me first.*

*It will no longer be just the two of you . . .* I continued. But this time, I could not reach the woman. Why? She had fallen in love with the promise of a child. In love? In love? What is love anyway? I could not win over her desire to be a mother. Three of them, Cain, Abel, and little Eva. Bang! Bang! Bang! One right after the other. It had taken me eons to get their parents to mess up. How long would it take to corrupt the trio?

However, Cain solved that puzzle for me. He greatly aided in my understanding of humankind. Who was Cain? A man obsessed with finding a secret to eternal life. Actually, he wanted to find an alternative to life in Eden as Adam had described it to him. He wanted to halt the process of dying. He feared his eventual death.

Death itself was a mystery. I did not know what it meant. The humans did not know either. So like Adam, Eve, and Abel, Cain's brother, Cain feared the unknown. Unlike the others, Cain wanted to do something about it. Cain wanted to retrieve the promise of life forever, even if he had to find a solution all by himself. Cain was Adam's first son, the first agriculturalist and naturalist—more devoted to plants than to people. My kind of scientist.

When Adam explained to Cain, his elder son, how events in the Garden had led to Eve and his eviction and a death sentence, Cain immediately became obsessed with finding ways to sustain life. How do I know he was obsessed? I am the author of obsession. I suggested his obsession to him, and he accepted it.

I listened and watched Cain as he examined the soil from which his father had been made; he sampled fruit and vegetables that his parents had taught him to eat and other plants that his parents had never sampled. He examined the roots of the plants and trees and became convinced that "certain plants" could be instrumental in sustaining life because of their connection to the soil from which his father had been made. He theorized that sustenance of life came via the soil, and somehow the edible roots of the trees and the plants were the key to prolonged life. Therefore, in Cain's way of thinking, the harvest from the Earth was far more important than any cooked flesh of the animals that Creator had told Adam to use as offerings to obtain forgiveness for transgressions. In essence, Cain wanted to thwart Creator's edict.

Here was a man I could use! He had his father's passion and his mother's obsession. Would many humans be like Cain? He solidified my original idea that food would be an ideal tool to bait humankind. I also learned from him what is meant by *obsession.*

Wow! *Obsession*! What a marvelous word!

What a marvelous tool! Cain did not look to Creator or ask His assistance or even ask for answers to his question: How can I live forever? Cain wanted to find the solution himself. A human who wanted to be independent of Creator! The evil that I have become, I accomplished by my own merits. Ways to deceive humans, I learned from mankind. Cain was one of my teachers!

Oh, cunning Cain! On, innovatively inspiring Cain! He taught me a lesson better than the one I learned from his mother. Wow! *Cain thinks he can find answers all by himself; Cain believes he does not need Creator!* I support that attitude. *Hooray for Cain!*

Before I tell you what happened next, I must give you a little background, information that you may have thought about but not "truly" digested. (Do humans ever understand anything? I wonder.)

After the original couple was evicted from their first home, Creator instructed them on how to atone for their disobedience—blood sacrifice of certain animals. The sacrifice of the animal was three fold. First, they received forgiveness from Creator. Also, the skins of the animals sacrificed were used as clothing. By sacrificing, the couple learned to cook meat. Yeah, yeah, yeah! Another rule. No eating raw meat.

*Blood sacrifice, hum. Something to keep in mind for future reference.*

So how do I carry out my plan to free the Earth of humans? I listened and learned from humans.

From their parents, I had learned that food is a doorway by which I could tempt the trio to do as I wanted. For some unknown reason, whether hungry or not, humankind was fascinated with food.

I also observed that Cain was obsessed with growing edible plants and vegetables, cultivating and replanting, growing and sampling these. Abel, on the other hand, was fascinated with livestock. He enjoyed leading sheep to green pastures, and he ate of the tender calves and kids. As they grew into manhood, and Eva grew into a most beautiful young woman, there was something else I learned. If Creator fashioned a woman especially for Adam, the two young men must need a woman too. And there was only one!

Because Cain was the oldest, he was promised Eva as his mate. Adam made the promise to his first-born son, but Eve felt differently. Although her son Cain was a freethinker, as she had been during her days in the garden, she, after becoming a parent, had become very careful about her children's future. She saw the need for their obedience to Creator. Her son Cain did not. So she knew that Abel, her obedient son, would make the better mate for Eva. He was like his father, Adam, focused and obedient, but I preferred Cain. As Eve had been in the garden, Cain was now my kind of guy, my kind of human.

Two things happened. Only one I orchestrated. I started making suggestions to Cain about his brother Abel. *There is only one woman available for mating*, I whispered. *There are two of you*, I continued. Cain's spirit was open to my suggestions.

Immediately, he became possessive. He declared his rights as the first born to have Eva as his mate. He resented even the conversations that Abel had with their sister, but the girl was captivated with the flocks that Abel cared for. She often followed Abel about as he led the flocks to pastures for grazing or to streams for watering. Cain's experiments with plants were only of minor interest to the sprightly young girl. She talked of nothing else but the beauty of the lambs. Right before the special sacrifice, Able presented a perfect ewe lamb to her as a gift, and Cain brought an assortment of fruit and vegetables. She was grateful for both gifts, but she treasured the lamb.

On the day assigned by Creator for them to offer sacrifices to receive forgiveness for any wrongful acts committed, the men, Adam, Cain, and Abel, prepared their offerings. Like his father, Abel offered young tender lambs from the flocks Abel tended. Cain, on the contrary, presented an assortment of vegetables and roots he had dug from the ground and fruit he had picked from the trees. Creator applauded the offerings of Adam and Abel, but critiqued and rejected Cain's sacrifice. Creator was patient enough to explain the reason for the rejection, yet Cain was angry.

I watched their ceremonies from my hiding place, a clump of sycamore trees, several leagues away. Because the heavenly hosts were nearby watching too, I could think of no reason why I should be absent and miss the festivities! When I saw the angry scowl on Cain's face, I knew I had a way in. I only need wait to catch Cain unrepentant and alone.

My wait was not long. Dejected, unrepentant, and alone sat Cain that very night. The exact conditions that opened the intellect to my persuasions. Although I would no longer take the shape of one of the animals to talk face-to-face with Cain, I had learned the power of psychic suggestions. As he tossed and turned in an uncomfortable sleep, I reminded him of his toil in the fields, of his planting and replanting, grafting new plants and fruits, cross pollination of berries and vegetables—such great ideas, and all for nothing. No one respected his chosen profession and the quality of his produce. Creator only respected blood sacrifices.

*And what about the girl?* I interjected. *Surely now, Adam may consider giving her to Abel, your brother. After all, his sacrifice has Creator's stamp of approval.*

Cain woke up angrier than when he had fallen asleep! He headed for the pastures just to have a chat with his brother. Lo and behold, who else was there? Eva! She was at the back of the herd running about chasing the stray sheep back into the flock.

"*What are you doing here?*" Cain growled at his sister. "*Go back to Eve's tent where you belong!*" As I listened to the tone of Cain's voice, I knew I had made my mark.

*Sick him! Sick him*, I roared to the horde of fallen angles who were loitering watching the humans. Faster than human winks, the countless hordes zoomed into the space occupied by Cain. They flew in and out, up and around as they collectively whispered devious commands to him. Their slurred words and garbled suggestions crescendoed into torrents of hideous cries. They tripped over themselves as they continued to suggest hateful phrases, lustful words, and spine-chilling suggestions. They gyrated; they mimed and demonstrated hideous lewd acts upon each other. In the realm of the spirits, their voices reached a thousand decibels. So loud were they that their cries caught the attention of the holy angels, but the holy angels could only watch the charade of the fallen angels. For Cain's attitude and actions had invited us, not them!

Well, a row ensued. *Cain, look over there! Pick up the stone, Cain! The stone!* And Cain listened and obeyed me! So Cain the stronger pounded Abel's head with the stone over and over until red liquid flowed from his head, nose, eyes, and mouth. Liquid like that which flowed from animals Creator told them to sacrifice. And then the blood stopped, and so did Abel's moaning. Was Abel dead? Yes, he was.

When Cain killed his brother Abel, fallen angels rallied. They cheered my progress and hailed me as their infamous leader. I had triumphed! I had finally learned how to influence humans to kill, but something stranger happened still.

Our celebration halted abruptly as Abel divided into two equal forms, each exactly like the other, only one lay still on the ground while the other moved about! Abel was now in two places. I saw him and I saw his frame. What was going on? Another lesson. Abel had entered the world of the spirits. Creator's angels came and took away the form that moved. Could it be that Abel had a spirit? And if so, where was it taken?

Cain placed Abel's frame under the ground. How many parts to a human? One? Two? Perhaps more! And if two or more, how would the supernatural parts of humans impact the spirit realm in which I live? Here was a mystery that neither humans nor I understood at that time. I would perfect the art of murder! For now, I partially understood what death meant.

So this was the death of a human. Cain was partially aware of it too, but he could only see the carcass. Alas, too late! I now recognized my power to steal, kill, and destroy. I nearly stole Cain's sanity when I influenced him to murder his brother, Abel. Abel's death was a potential to destroy the unit as they now called themselves. Cain had killed his brother. I had learned how to mastermind the murder of humans! The kingdom of darkness could now prove to be a potent threat to the kingdom of light!

# CHAPTER VI

Murderer? Slanderer? Who me?

You still do not believe that I have the power to influence human behaviors, do you? Whether you do or not makes absolutely no difference to me whatsoever. Nevertheless, for bragging rights, let me say this.

Think. If a hypnotist with limited training, let's say between one to twenty-five years, can successfully hypnotize a willing subject to behave as the hypnotist suggests, how much more can spirit beings as powerful as I influence a mere human? Think about it.

Do not compare a human's limited capacity to my supernatural capabilities. Any comparison of humans to me, I resent. I have learned overtime that most of humankind cannot think any higher than their sordid puny surroundings. Therefore, they either overestimate my powers or underestimate my influence. What I hate most about humans—and I do hate each and every one of them—is their puniness of spirit. Scrawny, drab, spoiled twits, the whole bunch of them, even those who claim to worship me. Worship, you ask? Devil worship? Why not?

Wickedness abounded on the Earth as I excelled in trickery! I was never so busy. Sinning was becoming an art form! Humans were multiplying at a hefty pace. Were they ever sinful! Wow! Every word out of their mouths was tainted with profanity and falsehood. Yet in the midst of an ocean of iniquitous behaviors, unsuspecting humans would darn cloaks of "rightness" and take a stand against my kingdom. Creator always had a mouthpiece! Since I did not plan to lose my bid for Earth, I employed every fallen angel to undermine Creator's spokespersons.

For example, a guy called Enoch, a grandson five generations removed from the "twit" Adam. Enoch irked me to no end. Moreover, he confused me. I thought I had corrupted every living soul. Apparently, I hadn't.

My outright ploy was to convince every human that sin is relative; that is, wrong and right are matters for each human to interpret. Sacrifices to Creator were at an all time low since its introduction in Adam's days. Why offer a sacrifice to cover sins if each human had his own definition of sinfulness?

In addition, who said there was only one ruler of the universe any way? I was propagandizing that my position as potential ruler was viable! My campaign slogan: *How could one ruler be present in so many different places at the same time? Surely, He needs help!* Hence, humans were incited to make their own objects of worship, gods of gold, silver, iron, bronze, and wood. They carved these and placed them in prominent places. How did their gods perform? *Ha, ha.* I used one fallen angel after another to fool humans into thinking that their idols could in fact help them.

Did I not declare that humans are gullible? In the world of spirits, my hordes and I spent countless hours reenacting the antics of humans as they bowed down and worshipped their idols. We laughed in the comic theater of the damned. The unending animated hilarity among demons started when humans expressed sincere devotion to these material gods of gold, silver, and stone, and erected monuments to these. Humans constructed extravagant temples, instituted modes of worship, and employed priests to offer sacrifices to their idols. Was this practice laughable or what?

Still the more sacrifices offered to nonexistent deities meant fewer sacrifices offered to Creator! Was I ever on an ego trip! I took for granted that I was only steps away from total triumph.

However, Enoch did not play by my rules! While other humans were invoking evil spirits to do their bidding or calling upon idols for help, Enoch called on Creator. He believed what Adam, his ancestor, told him about the power and rightness of Creator. This information Enoch shared with others. Hell had a problem. My orders to the host of darkness: *Take Enoch down!*

After years of tricking and deceiving men and women close to Enoch, I was primed to spring the trap to take his life. Just as I had orchestrated the demise of Abel, I had fortified hostile and murderous enemies against Enoch. Unbeknownst to him, I had influenced his enemies to lie in ambush one evening as Enoch took his daily stroll through the woods. Armed with stones and axes, six men stooped as they hid behind trees waiting for Enoch to pass by. The plan I had so tirelessly whispered to them was to kill him and hide his body under a mesh of dried leaves deep in the forest. My hordes continued chanting the chorus: *Kill him; kill him; kill him as* they hovered over the vagabonds. I sat in the stratosphere as look-out.

As Enoch walked alone on a path that led to certain death, he was joined by a bevy of Creator's angels who came out of nowhere and joined Enoch on his stroll. *Where did they come from?*

My gang and I stepped back, for we could see a band of angels in close file, surrounding Enoch. To my human sycophants, the angels were invisible. Yet they did not make a move towards Enoch because they sensed something most unusual that caused them to abort their plan to murder. There Enoch was; then he wasn't.

In the world of the spirit where I dwell, it was obvious what happened. One minute Enoch and the angels were walking along, and the next second Enoch was in Heaven. Imagine that! Creator's angels literally snatched him out of my grasp! The humans stood with bulged eyes and opened mouths as they saw Enoch gradually walk from Earth upward until he disappeared in the clouds. How do I know what they saw? They animatedly discussed it over and over! They did not mention an escort of angels, however.

Was I ever ridiculed that day! The pack from hell laughed me to scorn. Those disloyal fallen angels doubled over, frolicking as they laughed at me. They pointed their grimy fingers in my direction and snickered endlessly. They bandied about pretending to be humans, enacting what had just taken place. With an army like this, it is no wonder that Creator's angels stepped in and out unchallenged. How could I ever win with these? My hatred of the fallen angels soared to an even greater level!

Creator had spoiled the plot! My ploy to take out Enoch, the pious lunatic, was completely ruined. Creator's angels merely scooped down, picked up Enoch, and escorted him to Heaven. Enoch was not even dead! I thought they were only supposed to transport spirits that were separated from their dead hosts, not live bodies! How can I possibly triumph when something like that can happen?

I wanted to debate the issue. But—what could I say? You win some; you lose some. What action Creator sanctioned just to save that miserable human! Are there no hard and fast rules in this game when it comes to humans?

Nevertheless, I persisted in my efforts to destroy.

Revelry was the order of the day. At my insistence, the hearts of humans became grossly wicked. Every evil I communicated, humans sanctioned.

Humans discovered fermented beverages that made them drunk, so drunkenness was rampant. I applauded this discovery of beverages, which I labeled "spirits," for when humans were in a state of drunkenness, they were more susceptible to my influence.

Even other fallen angels made a phenomenal discovery. These beings discovered that fallen angels could choose to take on human forms. As my horde and I observed the antics of humans from our invisible world, thousands of fallen angels desired to live lifestyles of errant humans. Moreover, beautiful women were numerous and fallen angels lusted after these women too. Marriage to human women meant that fallen angels had to assume human forms. So millions opted to take the form of men in order to mate with women, joining humans in wantonness.

Why? Fallen angels were masters of corruptions. Having human forms gave them license to act out their obsessions. It was exactly what those imps craved since our garden days.

When angels first mated with humans, these kept their extra-terrestrial status secret. Not even their wives knew. Then unusually large babies were born to the women. Some of the babies were so huge that their mothers could not deliver and died in childbirth. The surviving children grew into giants. Naturally, offspring of angels were admired by the human race. *Hum. Human race? Angel-human mixture?*

Initially, I found the new breed offensive and inferior to angelic beings, but after pondering the possibilities of what continuous breeding among humans and angels might produce, I recognized a phenomenal possibility! Million of hybrids of humans and fallen angels! With enough mixing, future generations would no longer be fully human, would they? Surely, dehumanization of humankind was not Creator's intent!

Preoccupation with human sensuality had seduced fallen angels into unions that produced children who were angel-human hybrids. These in turn corrupted other humans, thus contributing to the kingdom of darkness.

In human forms, fallen angels exaggerated human actions. An ordinary human would drink and get drunk; angel-humans took drunkenness to exaggerated heights. Drunkenness encouraged them to commit lewd and lascivious acts on humans and animals. Regular humans ate to excess and often times became obese. Angel-humans eating habits ventured beyond gluttony. Lawlessness inspired the populace to do whatever their intellect imagined.

Congratulations were in order! I had aided humans in crafting a perfect environment in which evil could thrive unfettered! I danced the gig! I had a chance to command, even if only a world of semi-humans. Half angels! Half humans! And a future race of inhuman Earth dwellers! Wow, what possibilities!

By the time Noah came along, the entire race of humankind was just steps away from being totally defiled with the blood of fallen angels. I had no clue why Noah, his wife, his three sons and their wives were the only ones untainted. Getting my grip into Noah and his family might just mean triumph for the kingdom of darkness. Tainting the blood of Noah and his family became priority in my kingdom of darkness.

What was the big purpose in getting our grips into Noah? He needed to be silenced. He was a mouthpiece for Creator. He was forever yelling about what Creator wanted versus how the inhabitants were living. Noah's family was the only one without angel's blood, if there was such a thing. They were untouched by the alien pretenders, human impersonators.

The abdication of countless fallen angels to become pretend humans had decreased my invisible army, but a new and far more evil visible force was now at work in my service. These impressive new "humans" were far more convincing than the average human sinners were. Lawlessness became the order of the day. I need not bother about expending energy creating havoc in the lives of humans. It was being done automatically! Fallen angels were now intermingled with humans!

When the "eccentric" Noah first caught my attention, I was able to recognize that he had a connection to Creator that no other human had had up to that time. He lived in the city named for Adam. I set up shop there because Noah started preaching sermons about the end of the world, so he needed watching.

Now really? Do you think I would just sit still and let him be heard? Oh, no. Not in a million years!

The traits that Noah exhibited were similar to those of Adam who had been brought down by a woman, but then Adam had no choice of mates. Noah did. He chose a wife who listened to him and not to my hordes or me. Darn!

So I devised an extraordinary trap to ensnare Noah. I went after the most vulnerable member of his family. I purposed to ruin Noah through his son, Ham. I went after the youngster, as I had never targeted another human thus far. For at this juncture in my history, I had perfected my skill of deception. Moreover, I was coining a race of my own, human-angel hybrids.

Why did I target Ham? Simple. He was Noah's middle child, filled with uncertainty, wanting to obey his father, but at the same time curious about the lifestyles of the young men of his day. Also, he was fairly handsome and caught the eyes of the ladies.

The daughters of the match between fallen angels and human women were equally as beautiful as their mothers were, but were bigger in stature and stronger than ordinary women were. One of the hybrid girls became Ham's childhood friend. Am I cunning or what?

Friends fell in love. As a teenager, Ham asked Noah to ask the girl's father for her to become his bride. However, Noah, the dud, refused. Ham struggled with Noah's decision, but was placated when his father chose a bride for him. He was married four days before his family entered a floating zoo.

Noah and his sons walked the streets making their final appeal to the inhabitants to change their lifestyles and to come and join his family in the ark, a crude wooden structure that resembled a three-story temple. Noah let them know that he had extra room, because he had spent over a hundred years building the floating house. He was ridiculed and scorned.

In the invisible world, fallen angels chuckled, and in the visible realm, human-angel hybrids laughed outright. I roared deprecating belly laughs every time Noah mentioned a natural rainstorm. How was it possible to transfer an experience from the invisible world to the visible world? A rainstorm? What an imagination!

From time to time in the spirit realm, fallen angel had affected the elements, sun, moon, stars, caused clouds to form, which produced moisture. But as yet, no water had ever fallen upon the natural Earth. Humans had heard neither of rain, nor of the word *flood* that Noah kept emphasizing, for it had never rained in the natural realm. Even I had no clue about the gravity of what Noah was predicting. *What was a flood anyway?*

When Noah went to preach his final pre-flood sermon, his sons accompanied him. The sermon was delivered on a much-traveled thoroughfare. Angel-tainted and fashionably painted, four women stood among the disgruntled audience of men. No one responded to Noah's pleas to alter his or her lifestyle and join him and his family in their floating temple.

Among the crowd, Ham recognized his first love, but he avoided making eye contact with her.

What were my hordes doing as Noah proclaimed disaster to the unresponsive hearers? Yelling and screaming obscenities. In the natural realm, angel-humans equaled the fallen angels' cursing filthy expletives.

Under my tutelage, these hybrid women were primed to ensnare Noah in a sexual trap, and if not Noah, they were sanctioned to go after his sons, Shem, Ham, and Japheth. The hybrid women were equally as gorgeous and as strong as the hybrid men were, but these women hid their prowess from everyone except their fathers because they wanted to appear as human females of their day.

After Noah's unsuccessful plea, four beautiful women, hybrid offspring of fallen angels and human women, lay in wait for Noah and his sons. They stood prone in an alleyway off a narrow dirt road; their bodies pressed flat against the stone structures of four of the hovels in the alleyway. Their mission: seduce or kill.

Actually, I preferred seduction, but the death of these men would signify that not one of Adam's offspring remained, that humans were no longer—human! My hordes and I watched from behind the hovels near the square.

As Noah and his sons walked toward home, they were assaulted by the hybrid women whose strength surpassed theirs. One lifted Ham from the ground, twirled him round and round above her head, and then tossed him into the shrubberies. His father and brothers were repeatedly punched and battered about and were likewise lifted and tossed into nearby bushes. With unfeigned glee and much revelry, the women cheered each other on as they laughingly toyed with the men who seemed puny to them. As Noah and his sons got to their feet and ran for their lives, the women chased them. The chase ended when the men reached the city square where several lanterns cast beams of light into the doorways of houses. Voices were heard. The women abandoned the chase.

What would it take for Noah to realize that he would never convince the inhabitants that Creator's way was the way to go? A planet filled with lawlessness was exactly what I wanted and exactly what I got!

Finally, the odds seemed stacked in my favor. I screamed, *Got ya*! Can you imagine it? Millions of . . . , well, whatever—all of them evil! I awaited the outcome. Only one family to take down. The rest of Earth's inhabitants existed in a state of abomination. Boy, were those people evil! Their lifestyles indicated that the kingdom of darkness would triumph! Earth had become a den of wantonness. Sexual immorality, impurity, debauchery, idolatry, witchcraft, hatred, discord, jealousy, fits of rages, selfish ambitions, dissensions, factions, envy, drunkenness, and orgies. Wow! There were no restraints at all!

There again was that recognizable wall of holy angels as Noah and his family ran into the ark for safety. *Holy angel activity again!* My hordes and I backed away from the ark as far as possible to avoid a fight, but still see and hear what was going on. An angry mob pelted the makeshift fort with sticks and stones as they yelled ridicules. In the realm of the spirit, one of Creator's angels shut and barred the door to the ark.

*What was Noah going to do? Hide in there from the crowd forever?* My hordes and I reveled in the mockery of Noah by his neighbors and the crowd to whom he had preached for many human years! In the natural world, those undisciplined hybrids were in a state of merrymaking. For six days straight, the crowds gathered in front of Noah's wooden vessel to see if he and his family would exit. When they did not come out, the crowd yelled obscenities in the direction of the ark and hurled rocks at the structure.

*"There! That will teach you to criticize us, you outdated water bag!"* One mocker screamed, as he threw another rock at the edifice.

Each day the crowd lessened, and on day seven, no one showed up, but my hordes and I did. We had maintained our cover away from Creator's angels for all that time and continued to do so. The angels of Creator still held their positions around the ark where Noah and his family were. With the populace, it was a return to business as usual—marriages, merrymaking, drunkenness, and violence. It was day seven; the day the aforementioned flood began.

Which number lesson was this?

My hordes and I watched unobserved as water

gushed up from the ground and as it poured down from the clouds. The wall of holy angels remained intact surrounding the ark as the waters came up on the Earth. Day after day, the waters increased. Oh, those foul-mouth merrymakers were not so merry now! They climbed up onto roofs and on treetops and on hilltops and finally onto mountaintops. Then they could climb no further.

I watched and cheered as one human after the other drowned. My hordes and I rallied around the fallen angels who had taken on the form of humans to see what would happen to them. It was a learning experience to witness the drowning of each fallen angel that had taken on human form. Immediately after its body drowned, up popped a hideous demon. Monstrosities after monstrosities, grotesque, hideous, cankered, cancerous, twisted, and malformed. Scaly, scabby, fiery-eyed, sulfurous breath, slimy-tongued, slithery forms—evil and ugly, ugly, ugly! Yet the wall of angels that encircled the rag-tag floating house remained steadfast.

I sat in midair inundated by water. What living things remained alive after the deluge? Noah and his family, the animals he had spent 125 years collecting for his floating zoo, the insects and bugs that pestered the animals, the microbes that made their homes in the wood of the ark, and creatures that lived in water.

I wanted all humans dead! However, I wanted to arrange their demise. If it had been my choice, I would have preferred to have a new breed of human, those mixed with fallen angels, so that I could fly into the face of Creator to declare my kingdom had come, that I had won. Later I would have destroyed the miserable bunch of half-humans in, oh, so many bizarre ways as I lured them into destroying each other. I wanted them dead, but I wanted to do it my way!

Creator went to great extremes to save the human race. Noah and his wife, his three sons, and their wives were kept alive. Noah's family would be able to reproduce and fill up the Earth with people once again. A new group of humans loyal to Creator. I would have to start all over!

Pouting might be unbecoming for a character such as me, but I pouted! Why wouldn't Creator let me have the Earth whose inhabitants had voted Him out by their actions and corrupted lifestyles? He just could not leave bad enough alone! I knew of Creator's piety and love for the humans stretched farther than my mere satanic mind could fathom, but I never would have even guessed in millions of years to what limits Creator would resort to preserve a people with such propensity for riotousness, deception, and murders. These were my kind of humans, not His! Humans were proving to be deceptive rascals who would eventually prove they are not worth saving! Could He not see that?

I had no clue about the gravity of what Noah was predicting. For over a hundred years, I laughed at Noah, fallen angels ridiculed him, and humans tormented this lone purveyor of obedience to Creator. I knew Creator had something "up His regal sleeves," but I never fathomed that He would destroy everyone except His "pet," Noah, and Noah's family! I saw the signs, but I did not deduce. How could I have known? I was too busy rallying the hordes and gloating over the corrupted behaviors of Earth's inhabitants. My focus was on winning at all cost. I thought I had a chance of winning just this once!

The flood affected not only humankind; it practically devastated my kingdom. The physical body of every fallen angel that had taken on human form drowned. The spirits of these "angel-men" became disembodied spirits, actually demons. These could no longer materialize as men, but became hideous, ghastly beings. Evil these remained, but never again could these appear as men. These could only possess humans if allowed.

I now commanded demonic forces that even I found ugly and repulsive. Ugh! These demons spend most of their time challenging my authority! Payback? Don't bet on it!

Eight humans on the face of the Earth, a depleted army of fallen angels, and an ugly, smelly, crude batch of undisciplined demons. I don't know who felt worse, Noah or I? Actually, I was right back where I had started. No progress to show for so much effort.

# CHAPTER VII

So what happened next? Those dastardly demons tried to usurp my authority! The crude, rude, ugly bunch tried to undermine my kingdom! They tried to operate independent of me!

After Earth was significantly repopulated, demons took a liking to the plain of Jordan in and around the twin cities of Sodom and Gomorrah and refused to travel elsewhere. They had grown accustomed to stationary posts because these had once inhabited human flesh. These mutant fallen angels craved two things: to remain in their comfort zones and to live inside of humans again. Detestable! Unruly! A worst group could not be found!

Let me clarify something. There is a hierarchy amongst my hordes. The least important are demons because these are just plain dumb. They were not created; they were mutated—a bunch of dumb fallen angels too stupid to get out of their own way. Before the flood, they had opted to take on human forms to marry humans. When the flood came, the bodies that they occupied drowned. Thus, they became disembodied spirits, no longer able to materialize without the use of human forms. They spend all of their time trying to re-enter human forms because they are fascinated with humans and human vices. A sorry group of human wannabes. They have no direction, no purpose. They follow my leadership because they are too dense to come up with any ideas of their own. I loathe this bunch of scatterbrains—meddlesome, bickering, undisciplined disembodied spirits, dull enough to have been caught vulnerable in human flesh. I tell them what to do, step-by-step; they report back to me word-for-word. Evil initiative they do not possess; they are usually the first to retreat in spiritual warfare. Demons are an embarrassment even in the kingdom of darkness!

So after the flood, I was not about to have a group of renegade demons, so I acquiesced to their demands. I allowed them to operate in areas where they were comfortable, and in return, these committed to infiltrating the bodies of as many humans as possible.

Why force this group to accompany me? They are limited in intelligence. I find their presence demeaning and offensive. They are repulsive and have absolutely no class, if you understand what I mean.

Am I prejudiced? Most definitely! Even in the ranks of hell, I maintain a semblance of hierarchy, and demons and sub-demons are given no respect at all. In the order of demons, first tier are comprised of disembodied spirits of fallen angels that chose to marry human women. The sub-demons are the disembodied spirits of their offspring. Actually, the dogs of darkness literally hate each other, but the ranks and files hate demons most! Demons even detest themselves!

So what's the story?

I allowed demons the opportunity to invade an area, and what did they do? Infiltrated the people for sexual purposes and sexual purposes only. What did I say earlier? Demons have absolutely no initiative—one-track intellect!

I got the reports from time to time that the inhabitants in the twin cities, Sodom and Gomorrah, were becoming more and more riotous. That report was a-okay! When I questioned the messenger demon to ask its strategy, it answered, "*Sex.*" Mission? *Purpose? Procedure?* To all questions, that flakey demon answered: "*Sex.*" They had sent to me the dumbest of the dumb, the most stupid of the stupid, and the least creative of the dull!

*What happened to greed? Malice? Envy? Strife? Don't you promote those sins in Sodom and Gomorrah?* I yelled in anger. It just looked at me with its ugly face and answered, "*Yeah, but we are precise in what we do. The other demons said that I must say that we demons specialize. We do one thing, and we do that very well.* "

I arrived in Sodom the same evening as two of Creator's angels showed up. *What have these stupid demons done?* I asked myself, for I recognized the faces of the angels, and their presence meant war. They were in human forms operating in the natural realm.

My crew and I moved immediately to the shadows, under floorboards, and behind bushes and trees. If the angels knew we were present, they showed no signs of knowing. They moved about unconcerned.

A character, Lot, whose uncle was a constant "thorn" in my side, sat at the gate and greeted them. He invited them to spend the evening at his home. *Okay.*

The angels turned down Lot's invitation and declared that they preferred to spend the night in the square. *Not a good sign.*

However, Lot was so insistent with his offer that the angels gave in and followed him to his house. *What a relief!*

Meeting time. The hordes of hell convened on the plains next to the city of Gomorrah. *What's the status?* I asked the lead demon that I had left in charge. Here is what he answered me. "*In these cities, men no longer lay with their wives; they lay with other men. Women have no desire for their husbands; they prefer other women. There are no men in the cities who can escape our infiltration. Birthrates are at an all time low, and very soon there won't be any babies born at all.*"

*Okay . . .*

I flew back to Sodom for I knew that trouble was brewing. My hordes followed closely behind. I did not lead through the airways because other angels sent by Creator might be flying about up there, and I did not wish to encounter any of them. Instead, I flew as close to the ground as I could without touching the soil, slithering through shrubberies and trees, trying to remain in the shadows. The dogs of hell followed.

*In the first place, why were Creator's angels in the city? What was going on?* I could only be in one place at a time, and I depended upon daily reconnaissance reports to keep me apprised of what was happening in that region of the Earth. Ug! Demons! I should have known better than to leave them alone without stronger supervision!

I knew exactly where to find Lot. I followed the stench of sulfur. The stinking odor was emitted by hideous demons hiding nearby in alleyways and behind neighboring houses. Others encircled the foundation of Lot's dwelling. Some sat under the Earth right beneath the house. The demons were silent, but the horrid human men both young and old surrounded Lot's house, beating on the windows and doors, demanding Lot to send out his guests so that the mob could have sex with the men. Was that mob ever in for a surprise!

What did I do? My entourage and I sat behind a clump of trees in a wooded area across the way and watched from a distance. *Let the demonic scene unravel.*

*Do I challenge the angels? What for?* If only two angels were sent to deal with the city, it meant that their angelic prowess exceeded any force my hordes and I could muster.

Coward? Coward you say. Perhaps, but I choose my battles and that one I would let pass.

Well, out came Lot who had been rescued by

other angels in another city just months before. *What did this man have? His own contingent of angels ready whenever he was in trouble? It must have been that uncle of his, that Abraham. Abraham must have been praying for his errant nephew again!*

Lot appealed to the men whom he referred to as friends. *Friends? Were these the kind of friends Lot kept? If he kept friends like those, not even the prayers of Uncle Abraham should have gotten him out of trouble.*

Lot pleaded with the men to leave his guests alone and offered them his two daughters instead. Did they want the women? No. They demanded the men be sent outside.

Thus far, I had been upset with the demons that had orchestrated almost a total change in humans' sexual preferences. I envisioned the outcome. Just picture this—men cohabiting with men; women cohabiting with women. The result: fewer and fewer babies born. From a drop in population, to a lower population, to the lowest population, and eventually no humans at all. No births, no future generations. There just might have been some evil benefit to what the demons had instituted in the twin cities! Maybe the ghastly perverts were not as dumb as I thought!

A change of mind? No. I just wanted to observe the outcome.

Now you might suspect that my hordes and I would provoke a fight to promote the kingdom of evil. Oh, no! You don't realize who those angels were. They could easily have devastated the contingent I had with me. Even with the concentration of demons in that area, we still would have suffered defeat. The demons would have been the first to retreat, for they are genuine cowards.

Well, the orgy-seeking mob pressed together and progressed to the steps of Lot's house where Lot stood. They screamed out insults and threatened to have sex with Lot if he did not send the men out to them. *Poor fools. If they only knew.*

Just as the demon-possessed crowd was about to trample Lot as they strove to break down the door to his house, one of the angels reached outside and pulled Lot back into the house and shut the door. Moments after, the men nearest the door cried out because they could no longer see. The men were stricken with blindness. The angel's doing I surmised.

In our hiding place, the hordes started whispering among themselves. I shushed them, demanding that they be silent. I did not wish to draw attention to our position.

Lot came out again, but this time the mob was hushed and halted. He spoke to his two sons-in-law who were among the crazed men. I zeroed in on what he had to say. Lot warned his sons-in-law that they should leave the city because Creator was about to destroy the city. They laughed, then turned to the crowd and repeated what Lot had told them. The immoral crowd laughed Lot to scorn.

*Wait*! *Run that by me again. Did Lot say the*

word *"destroy"*? I asked my hordes. I took a few moments to analyze the situation.

*Let's see. Raphael and Gabriel showed up at Lot's house. Those two alone have the power to overpower the entire force that I have with me. I don't have time to send for reinforcements, neither are any of my posse brave enough to fly for help. Why should I call for help anyway? There just might be some value in what Lot said. More dead humans meant nothing to me.*

The cries from the blinded men must have diluted the men's sexual passions. For very soon after, the crowd disbursed. Silence reigned. No movement or sounds came from the house, the terrified demons stayed hidden, and my crew and I stayed in our hiding place. That night in the kingdom of darkness, demonic activities were at an all time low.

In the early morning before the rise of the sun, the angels were on the move. Gabriel held the wrists of Lot and his wife, and Raphael held the wrists of Lot's daughters. The family was being lead—almost forced—to the city gates, out of the city, and over the plains. It would have been simpler if the angels had lifted the humans and flown them out, but instead they held on to their charges and walked hurriedly, practically dragging the humans along.

My entourage of fallen angels and I followed at a considerable distance to see what the angels were up to, but those dastardly demons, refusing to follow, expressed relief that the angels had departed.

As the sun rose and Lot's family and the

angels reached the city of Zoar, the angels left them there. Then it happened. Not rain this time, but a rain of fire! It rained down burning sulfur on Sodom, Gomorrah, and the entire plain. The cities burned, the inhabitants burned, the vegetation burned. Oops! One member of Lot's family turned and looked back toward Sodom. It was Lot's wife. Her looking back did not matter to me, because she could not see us anyhow. Still, something bizarre happened to her! The woman turned to solid stone. Stone? Stone. The others walked on as if she had not existed. *Unnatural behavior for humans.*

So what happened to the stupid demons that inhabited the place, possessed, and oppressed the inhabitants? Most watched the destruction and cheered. Those levitating under the floorboards of Lot's house probably remained there long after the city was leveled by fire. Stupid, undisciplined, human pretenders!

My posse and I left the area. The disembodied spirits had no choice but to follow.

# CHAPTER VIII

I found myself lodged and discouraged in the Land of Oz some thousands of years ago when I came into contact with a man named Job. Creator was so fascinated with this man that Creator's confidence in Job disgusted me.

It was rumored in the world of the supernatural that a convention of heavenly angels was scheduled. I took the liberty to show up to represent all of the defrocked angels, those that would be out of place in heavenly settings. A visit was long overdue.

Since Creator holds no grudges, He treated me like a guest. I had no idea what was about to happen, but I found out that the topic of conversation was that man called Job.

When Creator asked my whereabouts, I answered that I had been up and down throughout the Earth. Then He asked me if I had observed His servant, Job.

Immediately, my defenses went up. *Job?* I said to myself. *Yes, I had noticed that Creator treated him favorably. So much heavenly protection for a mere human.*

I was respectfully yet devilishly elated when I was allowed to talk. *I mean no disrespect, but Job serves You for what he can get. Everything he touches turns to gold. You have angels surrounding him, his house, family, livestock—everything that he owns is under Your protection. I wager that if You destroy all that Job has, he will curse You to your face!"*

As I stood there in Creator's presence, I remembered the beating that Michael the archangel had given me, so I did not say anything further that might cause trouble. I shut up and waited to hear what Creator had to say.

Creator responded, "I give you power over all Job has. However, you may not touch his life."

After hearing those words, I left Creator's presence. Respectfully and hastily, I bowed my way out of Heaven, careful not to turn my back to Michael whose eyes never left mine. I spiraled downward, and on the way down, I rallied my troops. My mandate: Steal! Kill! Destroy!

I had been plotting Job's destruction for years. I was only hindered by the wall of heavenly angels that surrounded him, his family, and his possessions. That day the wall of angels opened, and Creator's angels stood aside as I walked through.

In the hearts of Job's rivals, the Sabeans and Chaldeans, I had long since planted seeds of jealousy. In one day, my plans for Job's destruction were implemented. *I plan ahead for opportunities such as this.*

The vicious Sabeans stole Job's cattle and killed all his herdsmen except one who relayed the disaster to Job. The brutal Chaldeans rustled Job's herd of camels and murdered all the camel drivers except the one who told what happened. My hordes and I sensed the electrical charges emitted in the air around the vicinity of Job's dwelling, and we persuaded his shepherds to lead the sheep to a field most probable to have a lightning storm. Just as I had calculated, lightning struck and killed Job's flocks of sheep and all of his shepherds except one who reported the disaster. The lightning storm was followed by a windstorm that destroyed the house of Job's eldest son, killing all of Job's children who were celebrating their brother's birthday. In one day, in a matter of hours Job was childless and penniless. My hordes and I stood in midair in the center of the devastation and roared with laughter.

So what did Job do? Instead of cursing Creator as I had predicted, he tore his robe, shaved his head, lay on the ground, and prayed to Creator. The twit actually thanked Creator for the time he was allowed to have the things he no longer owned.

The very nerve of the dimwitted human! He made me look bad! How could I show my face in Heaven again? Job was supposed to go under, not sing the praises of Creator!

I spiraled down to Earth. First stop? Uz, a thicket outside of Job's house. As I observed Job and listened to his conversation, I reflected on my past experiences with the dastardly humans.

After I received word of a follow-up angelic "workshop," I showed up in Heaven again. Basically, a similar conversation took place between Creator and me. He asked where had I come from and if I had seen his servant Job. My answer, *I come from walking up and down in the Earth, and yes, I have seen Job.*

"There is not another man in all the Earth like Job," Creator actually brags. "He lives righteously and avoids evil. Job is a man of integrity, yet you want to destroy him for no reason," Creator continued.

*Skin for skin*, I answered. *All that a human has he will give for his life. Job is no different from any other human*, I responded. *Once Job experience sickness, he will curse You to Your face.* Without saying so, I silently begged for a second challenge.

"Satan," said Creator, "You have permission to affect Job's health, but you shall not take his life."

So right away I exited Heaven, consulted with the dogs of hell, and set in place a trap that would result in cancerous skin sores. Do the math. Poverty plus lack of proper nutrient plus weeks and months of lying on the ground mourning in sackcloth and ashes, Job became afflicted with a rare case of dermatitis that produced boils all over his body. He itched day and night. When he scratched his skin with his fingernails, inflammation set in. To ease the itching, Job scraped his body with a piece of broken pottery. The abrasive dirty piece of ceramic produced further skin irritation, which resulted in puss-filled pockets of runny sores. Job's body was a mess! There was not one spot on his entire body including his head that did not have a runny sore.

A bombardment of oppressive evil spirits

tormented Job's wife with discouraging suggestions. Throughout the day and most of the night, demonic forces repeatedly suggested to her that it was best if her husband were to just "curse Creator and die." After a series of intense suggestive onslaughts, Job's wife accepted the suggestion of demons as her own and spoke the words aloud. Very early one morning, she spoke the words of demons to her husband.

"Job, she said, "If you are going to live in so much agony and pain, why don't you just curse God and die?"

Hooray for the kingdom of darkness! She spoke exactly what I wanted her to say. I wanted Job to believe the words his wife had spoken, since no force in hell seemed capable of getting Job to defame Creator. Perhaps his wife could.

However, did Job listen to his wife? No. Instead, he answered, "Do you hear yourself? Should I praise Creator only when He gives good things to me? Do I abandon my belief in Him when I am faced with bad times? You don't sound like yourself. These words are not yours. Have you been talking to some of your foolish friends again?"

*The wrong response, Job!* I shifted tactics to Job's friends, Zophar, Eliphaz, and Elihu.

For seven days demons of hell played with their psyche as they sat silently in Job's tent. Their space was inundated by spirits of self-righteousness. At the end of seven days, when they began to speak with Job, instead of offering comfort and support, Zophar and Eliphaz hinted to Job that all of his misfortunes had to be the result of a sinful lifestyle. Elihu angrily blasted Job, accusing him of justifying himself rather than Creator.

Did Job accept what his friends had to say? A thousand no's! He defended Creator and he defended himself. What would it take to destroy this guy?

What finally happened? Job prayed to Creator for his three friends and Job is cured eventually. His wife is happy once more, he fathered ten other children, and his wealth is restored. What happened to my plans for Job's destruction? Foiled!

All that trouble Job endured, and the "twit" didn't even know that I was the instigator!

# CHAPTER IX

*Listen, Kid, you are in Babylon, not Israel. You are captive, not free. You are supposed to do as you are told and be grateful to do so.* These are the words that I screamed at Daniel from the spirit realm, but he would not heed a word I whispered. Daniel did not hear me.

A few thousand years ago, a boy named Daniel was a thorn in my side, a fly in my evil "bowl of soup." I wanted him dead the day he was offered a position among the wise men of Babylon, and he refused to accept it. First, he simply declined the proscribed method of training because the Babylonian food was offensive to him. What made it offensive? He claimed that the food was unacceptable to Creator's laws. Daniel insisted that Creator's regime for healthful eating was best for him, and so his trainer acquiesced. The trainer should have forced fed Daniel!

Daniel could have been a major player in the kingdom of darkness. Clean cut, handsome, smart, with an aptitude for learning languages. So much talent that could be harnessed for evil.

From the day the name "Daniel" was brought to my attention, I set out to destroy the slick kid. I wanted him dead. Why? He would not budge one inch toward my kingdom of evil. A teenage miscreant, surrounded by a nation of astrologers, Daniel refused to become one. Instead of working magic or reading the stars, *Daniel* interpreted dreams. He refused to perform duties of a warlock or a fortune-teller or a diviner. Instead, Daniel boldly followed Creator's dietary laws, and he prayed to Creator three times a day. *Get a life!*

Daniel's stubborn disposition threatened my kingdom. You have heard about Nebuchadnezzar, haven't you? The whole world knew of him. He had a great passion for pillage and murder! An arrogant and ruthless king. My kind of ruler. Well, I toyed with the idea of using Nebuchadnezzar to destroy Daniel. With his beliefs, I could not allow Daniel to look good in the eyes of the king!

Anyhow, Nebuchadnezzar had a detailed yet disturbing dream he needed interpreted. The devious part? Nebuchadnezzar could not remember one iota of the details, yet the dream disturbed him greatly. Hence, he commanded his wise men to tell him the details of the dream and to interpret the dream as well. Ingenious!

When they were unable to interpret his dream without first knowing its content, King Nebuchadnezzar ordered their execution. *Wow! My kind of guy!*

If eliminating Daniel meant the death of every astrologer, soothsayer, palm reader, sorcerer in Babylonia, so be it! The more dead humans, the fewer I needed to kill! I just wanted Daniel dead.

What did Daniel do when he heard that all the wise men had been sentenced to death? He and his cronies prayed to Creator. The result? Daniel was able to tell Nebuchadnezzar the content of the dream and what the dream meant. How did he get the answer? You guessed it. Creator sent him the answer!

I was so undone! I kicked at golden statutes, silver pots, and iron balustrades. I swirled, swerved, and plummeted up and down in midair! Not just one dream was Daniel called upon to interpret, but he was frequently asked to decipher mysteries as well. I was so enraged!

Okay. Nebuchadnezzar eventually died, and Belshazzar, his son, became king. At one of his hedonistic feasts, Belshazzar and his guests drank wine from goblets pillaged from the Hebrew temple. The Hebrews deemed the goblets as sacred utensils because these had been dedicated to Creator.

As Belshazzar drank from the goblet, he praised images of gold, silver, bronze, iron, wood, and stone. I personally sat among his collections of gods. Fallen angels and I joined in the king's revelry. It was our kind of gathering. Even parasitic demons were busy trying to enter the molds of the drunken king, his nobles, and his concubines. Of course, "pristine" Daniel was not there.

In an instant, an angel of Creator's zoomed in and stood on the wall behind the king's throne. He wrote an indecipherable phrase on the wall. My hordes and I witnessed the entire event, for it took place in the spirit realm. However, the mystified, terrified partygoers saw only the hand as it wrote on the wall. They also saw the indecipherable message. Were they ever frightened!

The dogs of hell and I stood at attention. I pondered. *One angel? I could take one angel.* Yet if there was one angel in the palace, there might be thousands outside. It was not the time to provoke a battle that I might not win.

The king and his guests were a laughable bunch. The king paled, his knees locked, and he fainted temporarily. Some of his guest lost control of their bodily functions. Most of the celebrities urinated in their robes and liquefied excrement flowed down the legs of others. Urine and feces flooded the floor. Screams erupted from the vile women as well as from the mouths of cowardly men. Most grasped their stomachs and even more gripped their chests. All called on one god or another, and some prostrated themselves before the images of statues of gold, silver, bronze, iron, wood, and stone in the corner of the room.

My hordes placed their feet upon the heads of the terrified humans. They did not know that they were under the feet of fallen angels because the demonstration of angelic dominance occurred in the invisible realm. Surely, in the natural realm, the humans sensed the pressure of their subjugation.

Cowardly, the revived king promised wealth and power to anyone who could tell him what the writing meant. The magicians, enchanters, astrologers, diviners—none could decipher the message. So what did the pig of a king do? Heeded his wife's suggestion and called for Daniel. I screamed at him, *No! Give the magicians and enchanters a second chance! Ask the astrologers? Give them more time! The diviners could cook up an answer if they are given time to consult me! Give them time!* I screamed louder and louder. Alas, Beltshazzar did not sense my advice. Instead, he called for Daniel who interpreted the message on the wall.

What did the message forecast? The immediate death of Belteshazzar and a new reign by a foreign sovereign. Bloodshed and mayhem all in one night! This was my type of excitement!

My number one instrument in Babylonia, Belteshazzar, was killed in a bloody take-over of his kingdom. No loss. I had planned for his demise any way, but Daniel was supposed to be killed in the fray! He wasn't dead.

What happened next?

I set up headquarters in Babylon. Daniel needed watching. My hordes were given assignments throughout Persia, but reports were to be made to me in Babylon.

How do evil spirits tear down an upright human? Create an aura of jealousy among that man's associates, and they will do all in their power to defame and destroy that man, the object of their jealousy. My job is a piece of cake among jealous humans!

However, the new king, Darius, was not as wicked as I prefer kings to be. He was impressed with Daniel's credentials and planned to make Daniel prime minister. That would not do!

When word got out about Daniel's upcoming promotion, the malicious government officials were stroked by demons of prejudice. Jealous spirits intervened. Daniel's peers did not want him, a foreigner, to rule over them.

Demons of lust, greed, and jealousy surrounded the officials. Evil spirits fed them ideas about how to destroy Daniel. Demonic hordes screamed innuendoes and shouted criticisms of Daniel's management style. *How can he deal fairly with the citizens of Babylon?* Repeatedly, I reiterated. *After all, Daniel is different. He is an exile from another country. How dare he aim for so high a post in a country where he is not even a citizen! He doesn't even serve the gods of Babylonia.*

Finally, one addled brained official zeroed in on the actions I wanted the officials to take. *If a fault were to be found in obstinate Daniel, it would have to do with his service to Creator. Trap Daniel through his worship of Creator!* I transmitted suggestions as the humans hatched a plan.

You did not have to be a demon from hell to see through my plan. The government officials from the least to the highest agreed and recommended to Darius the king that he, Darius, should issue an edict forbidding prayers to any entity except himself. The ban on prayers to other deity would be for thirty days. Punishment for failing to abide by the decree: time spent in a den of lions. Darius, whose ego was significantly stroked by sycophants and lackeys, fell for the trick and signed the decree into law.

Of course, I infiltrated the minds of the officials, convincing them to spy on Daniel. I sat midair to watch Daniel personally. That stakeout was too important to be assigned to any other evil spirit. I wanted to take Daniel down.

I watched as Daniel opened his upstairs window, knelt facing east, and prayed to Creator. The trap was sprung!

My human hordes found Daniel asking Creator for help and immediately informed Darius, the king, and demanded that Daniel be thrown into a den of lions. Darius recognized the ploy, but it was too late. Darius' decree was irreversible. Daniel was thrown into a den of lions! A stone was placed over the mouth of the cave.

Hooray! Late night dancing in the kingdom of darkness!

Nevertheless, my celebration was short lived. For the entire night, one of Creator's angels stood between Daniel and the lions. The presence of the angel calmed the lions, so the animals did not tear Daniel into pieces as I had hoped they would! My plan for Daniel's death was foiled! There was no need to challenge the angel, for I knew I would not win against him either.

Some time later, I spotted an angel flying toward Daniel's house. Irate, I attacked the angel. For twenty-one days we fought, face-to-face, sword to sword. The fight reminded me of the brawl I had with

Michael. This angel was no Michael. I was strong enough to challenge that angel. We fought day after day, night after night. I refused to allow the angel through to reach Daniel with answers to prayers.

What finally happened? You guessed it!

Michael came to help the angel. The angel got by me and through to Daniel. I got a second beating. Daniel received an extended glimpse into the spirit realm. He was told by the messenger of Creator's what was written in the Book of Truth.

At that point, I needed to move on. I assigned a fallen angel as prince over the area to control the demons that preferred to reside there. There was no longer any use in my trying to destroy Daniel. Creator won the day.

# CHAPTER X

Five, four, three, two, one. The countdown from b.c. to a.d. reached zero. It was a New Year's party that I did not enjoy! It commenced Satan's stupid years, the devil's unproductive years, my "clueless" years. What was I clueless about? The whereabouts of the Promised One, code name, Adam II.

From Abraham to Joseph, the husband of Mary, I scrutinized possible redeemer types. I made educated guesses based upon the amount of angelic activities that took place in the universe at any given time. As I waited and watched, I continued my mission to steal, kill, and destroy.

When I suspected Abraham of being a possible progenitor of Adam II, I caused problems in his lifetime. Isaac followed in his father's footsteps, and he experienced some of his father's woes. My hordes spent many human years prompting Jacob, the younger of Isaac's twins to be deceptive and underhanded. In that case, I bet on the wrong twin. I persuaded Esau to marry women most unlikely to be in the line of progenitors of Adam II.

One particular night, I was called from presiding over a séance to spy on angelic hosts walking up and down a stairway to and from Heaven as they ministered to and protected the infantile, spoiled, cheat, Jacob. The unappreciative youngster thought he was dreaming, but he was allowed a glimpse into the realm of the spirits. I watched for hours as those angels moved up and down the staircase. Angels looked after Jacob, a cunning little twit who deserved destruction! Still, he was hedged about by angels.

All of Jacob's years in Haran and even on his journey home to Canaan, a wall of angels surrounded him and held fast. I stood over Rachel, Jacob's favorite wife, with intensions of killing his child as it entered the world. Instead, his wife succumbed to death. I plotted the corruption of Jacob's children, encouraged cowardice among them, and deceived some in to becoming murderers and assassins. I set loose demons of lust on a foreign prince, driving him to rape Jacob's only daughter, and provoked Jacob's sons to sell one of their own brothers into Egyptian slavery. Yet a wall of heavenly angels remained steadfast surrounding Jacob's bloodline. The presence of angels made no sense to me.

Even at Jacob's death, the wall of angels remained. Instead of dying, Jacob gave up the ghost voluntarily and moved freely from the natural to the supernatural. I stood waiting for Jacob to make his entrance into the world of spirits. I wanted my face to be the first that he saw as he stepped into the realm of the supernatural, but angels escorted Jacob back to Creator. Even in their deaths, I could not penetrate the wall of angels surrounding those I suspected of being progenitors of Adam II.

Busy, busy, busy was I!

As the potential generations increased in

numbers, I wreaked havoc on the people of the nations to whom Adam II was promised. I caused them to be despised and rejected by other nations. I proclaimed to the hordes of darkness that worldwide corruption was our intent, death to possible progenitors of Adam II was our initial focus, and eradication of humans in general was our primary aim. My instructions: *By any means possible, steal, kill, and destroy! Let's take them down.*

Who was Adam II? The secret was out, but no one was talking.

A famine I orchestrated in the days of Elimelech drove possible progenitors to the land of Moab. A most unlikely place for families to raise children, for many of the children in that land were burned as sacrifices to gods of Moab. Just maybe, the forefather of Adam II would pass through the fire and die there!

I drove jealousy into the hearts of the Hebrews to crave to be like other nations, to demand to have a king over them like neighboring nations. *Why should you have Creator ruling over you when you are not sure there is such a being?* I whispered in the ears of countless Hebrews. My motive? A king would form an army. With an army, the nation would fight wars. In wars, humans would die. Possibly in one of the battles, any remaining progenitor of Adam II would perish, and history as forecasted would be altered. Adam II could not be born!

The Hebrews asked for a king, and their king, Saul, became putty in the hands of evil spirits. He was frequently tormented by evil spirits and exhibited fits of rage. Eventually, I convinced Saul to fall on his sword and kill himself. Another door was closed to Adam II.

The moment King Saul was pronounced dead, I unplugged every stop to seek out and destroy his successor, David, who just might be a potential progenitor of Adam II. I had tried early in the young man's life to kill him, but he would not die. A lion, a bear, giants—none took him down. I masterminded a plethora of family problems: Betrayal by his favorite son, an unfaithful wife, murder, incest among his children—these should have driven him to use his sword to slit his own throat. Not so with this king. From time to time, a wall of angels surrounded him, and I could not take him out before his time.

A succession of murderous kings sat on the throne. Families were targeted for destruction; entire lines were wiped out. Still, nothing worked! I knocked down walls, stormed towers, and levitated in dungeons. I presided over beheadings and masterminded infanticide and murders. I questioned the validity of prophets. Is he the One? When in doubt, I ordered: *Kill! Kill!* Any entryway into a human's spirit, demons entered! Any device available for destruction, I used to gain leverage! If it were possible, I would have used the elements, the sun, moon, and stars. Whatever!

I enlisted followers, threatened demons, cajoled and promised humans anything. I frightened, horrified, terrified, mystified. I refused nothing and did everything. All to put an end to Adam II before his beginning, and nothing worked!

I found out thirty years after his birth that I had missed opportunities to kill him. Why? I did not know who he was! My intelligence was useless!

A girl named Mary received a message right under my nose. Legions of fallen angels trailed Gabriel when he soared through the airwaves. What happened? I could not be sure of the message; a wall of angels surrounded the girl.

I asked for an audience with Creator, for I wanted to argue the matter of free will. I was shocked when He bragged on the girl! "She is blessed among women, isn't she?" I nearly screamed and pulled on my angelic locks, but I dared not. "The girl has willed to keep evil out of her thoughts, her words, and her actions. You have no power over her. She has willed to obey Me. The wall of angels surrounds her and everything that pertains to her. She is covered by angels in answer to her prayers. You cannot touch her; her mind is closed to your suggestions, and she wills it that way."

In the past, there had been opportunities to grab momentary peeks, minute hints of what was going on in the minds of humans. However, for thirty years, my hordes and I could only make guesses. What hindered my agents? Impenetrable walls of heavenly angels. With every opportunity in the world to destroy a child, He survived!

I learned after the fact that the unsanitary con-ditions in the stable, where He was delivered, were sufficient to make Him ill. The hay upon which the woman gave birth was rippled with bacteria. Germs spread by flies that landed on the surface of the swaddling cloths He was wrapped in were enough to cause life-threatening infections. Yet the child survived.

Was it ineffective reconnaissance on my end?

If any one had information, it would have been Herod, king of Judah. He did my bidding and had all male humans two years and under killed in the vicinity I suspected as the birthplace of Adam II.

Every tidbit of Scripture that forecasted the birth of Adam II, I rehearsed. Every conversation that related to Him, I intercepted. Incessant movement, chaotic ramblings, fettering from place to place, swerving and swirling, going up and down, searching for signs in the skies, the Earth, the center of the Earth—I did it all! Still, I could not ascertain what was happening even though it was forecasted! I could not foresee! I had no confirmation! Confirmation comes from humans, and they were silent about Adam II. Or did the wall of angels cover their conversations too?

Nevertheless, the hosts of Heaven were unusually busy. My hordes and I spent most of our time docking and dodging, avoiding confrontations that we knew we could not win. Thousands of years anticipating, forty-two generations of plotting, and I missed my target! I blew it!

Do you want to know something else? I hold those stupid demons responsible because of their incompetent reconnaissance. If, as fallen angels, they had carried out their missions and not been so interested in the antics of humans, they would not have become the hideous, stupid, inept demons that they are! I loathe those beings. I would destroy them myself, but I am unable to put them out of their miserable existence! Dumb though they are, I still need them to keep eyes on dastardly sneaky humans.

As it stood, I was in for a battle. I had lost the war of the generations.

On the day the Teacher's wall of angels divided, the division was similar to the parting of the Red Sea. Hosts of angels, uniformly standing shoulder to shoulder, parted to open the wall. It was at His baptism by John. My hordes and I stood at a distance behind the rocks and hills, near the religious leaders whom we followed.

When the Teacher's hardheaded, no-nonsense, unrelenting cousin, John, revealed Him, I sat front row. After John baptized the Teacher, Creator confirmed my suspicion when He announced from Heaven, "This is my Son Whom I love. I am well pleased with Him."

*Too late*! demons screamed. *We found out too late!*

He had been made known, but the purchase had not yet been made. Blood sacrifice had not been offered. What would be the blood sacrifice? Thousands of lambs? I must find the flocks and orchestrate the death of the lambs. What about oxen? Doves? Whatever animal could be sacrificed, I must destroy through drought, famine—by any means! *Make sure you destroy sacrificial animals,* I commanded the dogs of hell.

Frustrated, I started grasping at straws. I followed Him into the desert and watched Him for forty days and forty nights. I needed time to observe Him. I had never heard Him speak; I had never suspected Him. He must be stopped! He must be destroyed. Now He had to be killed.

I cannot believe that I was stumped for so many years! How could He have escaped by sentinels? Now He was fully grown! Better if He had died an infant!

Was it Creator's plan to keep Adam II's presence on Earth hush-hush? I had been duped for so many years! How had Creator kept such a monumental event so great a secret in so vast a universe?

The Teacher became my personal assignment. I followed Him into the dessert. For forty days, I watched and observed Him. I needed time to study my opponent.

My assessment of Him*? Hmm. Tall, but not too tall. Shoulders? Could be broader. Not very good looking, not nearly as good looking as Creator made me. Unimpressive, except for those heavenly angels surrounding Him, following Him, standing near by, or lurking in the shadows. Clogging up the airways, they were!*

In the desert He ate no food, drank small portions of water only, and He prayed incessantly. *How long can He keep this up*? I asked myself.

Ten days passed. *He must be hungry*, I said to myself. Still He prayed. Twenty days passed. *He must be even hungrier*. Yet He prayed. Thirty days passed. Still He prayed. Where had I seen an attitude like His? Dejavue. He reminded me of persistent Noah, unshakable Job, and unwavering Daniel. The attitudes of those men bore holes in my theories about humankind. He behaved like all three, only more so. *Our mission: Watch this man. Let me know everything He does and especially what He says. Then I will ascertain whether He is Adam II,* I instructed the hordes of hell.

Forty days later, He concluded His fast.

*Surely, You must be hungry*, I said in a voice more impressive than when I spoke to Eve. *Creator says You are His Son. If You are, why don't You turn these stones into bread so that You can have food to eat?*

"It is written: Man does not live on bread alone, but on every word that comes from the mouth of God," was His answer. He actually quoted Creator after going forty days without eating! What was my defense against a man who used Creator's words as his offence?

I painted a hologram of the temple. He stood at its highest point. *Creator says that You are His Son. If You are, it would be a light thing for You to throw Yourself down so that His angels will catch You*, I prompted.

How did He answer? You guessed it. "Creator says that we are not to put Him to a test," I sensed the presence of the heavenly host in the background. I was two steps from flying away.

*Okay. Last try.* I produced Hologram Number 2. We stood on a high mountain, scenes of splendorous dynasties, kingdoms, empires—Babylon, Nineveh, Egypt, Indus, Israel, Medes, Persia, Greece, Roman, Inca, Aztec, Mayan, Mali, Songhai, China, Britain, America—kingdoms from past to present to future, one after the other were pictured on the walls of that mountain.

*I will give You all of what You see here if You would just bow down and worship me,* I appealed in my most elegant voice. My suggestion made Him angry.

"Get away from me, Satan!" He said sharply. "It is the words of Creator that He alone is to be worshipped and served!"

I knew the Person, but I did not recognize Him in the form of a human!

The heavenly angels that I sensed were nearby were now closing ranks around Him. I got out of the desert very quickly.

Immediately after leaving, I called upon the demonic hierarchy, fallen angels, principalities, powers to convene to plot a path of destruction for this would-be Adam II.

Only once was there activity of angels on Earth such as this. Thirty years prior. Angels—rigorous, full of light, busy, productively occupied. Angels, silent, bright, emitting brilliant beams of light.

I operated in panic—no announcement of

any convention in Heaven. If one was planned, I was not invited.

His protection? A wall of angels similar to walls of angels I had witnessed around Noah, Job, and Daniel. Only His hedge of angels was bigger, stronger. Angels I had not seen since my days in Heaven made up the ranks. These angels were stalwart, robust, strong, and more serious than serious. They were threatening, intimidating, yet obedient to Creator without question. Sides had been taken eons before, and I was well aware whose side these were on.

I kicked every demon that was within kicking distance. I pounded every defrocked angel that was within reach. I was enraged and started a fight among fallen angels.

I thought I was a master at guessing, yet I needed humans to confirm information. No one said anything, at least not the people whose conversations I listened to.

After His fast in the desert, no demon was safe in His presence! In a town called Capernaum, one Sabbath morning when He taught in the synagogue, there was a man possessed by a demon, an evil spirit. Instead of being quiet, the evil spirit drove the man to scream aloud at the top of his voice. *Aha! Why are You here? You have come to destroy us! I recognized who You are, the Holy One from Creator!* (Those dumb demons are forever drawing attention to themselves. They never learn!)

He demanded that the evil spirits be quiet and

come out of the man. Just like that. The dumb demons had no choice but to leave. It served them right.

One day as He stepped ashore in the area of Gerasenes, a demon-possessed man met Him at the shore. The demons I had assigned to destroy the man's mind had infiltrated his body and tormented him so that he wore no clothes and lived in tombs. The demons' job was to drive him to behave as an animal, and the man was just steps away from it.

*Aha! Why are You here? You have come to destroy us! I recognized who You are, the Holy One from Creator!* The demons yelled out. The condition of the man was a source of humor to the hordes of demons and fallen angels. The man was just one of my many subjects in experiments on the human psyche. I wanted to see just how many demons one human spirit could support. Twenty? A hundred? Perhaps a thousand or more? The man's body had been taken over by legions of demons. He had become hell's horrible sideshow! Humans chained the man's hands and feet repeatedly, but the many demons that possessed him gave him superhuman strength; he broke the chains every time. What a character he had become! Naked and screaming, he roamed the hills and valleys like an animal, providing demons with entertainment.

However, the Teacher (*and I was still guessing His identity*) showed up, and instead of running from Him, the demon-possessed ran to Him. He commanded the demons to exit the body of the man. And they did.

At another time, a man brought his only son to the new Teacher. The boy was tormented by demons that ravaged his body. My experiment? To watch the stages of demonic possession. When tortured by the repulsive demons, the boy screamed, threw himself on the ground, convulsed, and foamed at the mouth. What a hideous sight! This scene replayed periodically. Right in front of the new Teacher, demons inside of the boy put on a show! Stupid! Stupid! Stupid! The demons were ordered by the Teacher to exit the body of the boy, and they vacated pronto. What did I do? Nothing but watch as the hideous demons became even more repulsive as they joined me again in the spirit realm.

There was no stopping this Teacher, or so it seemed. He drove out mute demons, and the men spoke. He commanded demons of blindness to come out of their hosts, and the former hosts became sighted. The Teacher was on a mission, and if left unchecked, He would destroy my kingdom!

Killing John, who baptized the Teacher, became a priority in the kingdom of darkness. At his ministerial debut, I thought the Teacher might lay claim to being the next Messiah, so the order to kill Him went out immediately in the kingdom of darkness. Now that there were two of them, why not destroy the Teacher and John?

Influencing a human to kill John was "iffy." He was well liked by so many; his enemies were few. Even the worst among the people had respect for John. Since Herod the First, I had employed the Herods to carry out mass murders in their generations, but the current Herod Antipas did not hate John enough to have him killed. *Plan B. Trick the lewd, incestuous brute to carry out my plan.*

But Herodias, Herod's wife, ex-sister-in-law and half niece, hated John. Why? John openly spoke about the wrongness of their marriage. *Ha! ha!* There is nothing like an angry woman who could assist me in carrying out murder.

A plan was concocted. I whispered the plan to Herodias. She accepted my plan as her own, and she told her daughter. The daughter was to dance for Herod—what relations was Herod to her? Stepfather? Uncle? Granduncle? Anyway, she was to entice Herod with her dancing then ask him for John's head as a reward. She danced; then the ax-man got busy. John was beheaded.

Why? I suspected John as a claimant to Adam II. One down and one to go!

Who could I use to bring about Adam II's destruction? The common people loved Him! He looked after them. He healed their sick, repaired sightless eyes, and made cripples walk. He even raised people from the dead! I ought to know, for I was instrumental in orchestrating their deaths. Adam II, also called the Teacher, drove me to my lair, frustrated and clueless.

Demons hissed as my scheme took form. I summoned spirits of lust and greed to encircle and ensnare those who were close to Him, those miserable, smelly fishermen with their chronic addiction to low living, and the other pious yet doubtful of the bunch. When money was offered to turn over the Teacher, similar to the ploy used to discover Samson's weakness, only one of His followers took the bait. I had made headway! I would take Him down with the help of one of His own. In reality, I planned to kill them all, but I needed to kill the Teacher first.

Yet how could I set a trap for a man who walked in the realm of the natural and could command evil spirits in the supernatural? How could I tempt Him with wealth when He showed no interest in owning anything? How could I offer Him power when He possessed power already? Was I ever in a dilemma!

He surrounded Himself with regular folk. Where was the guile? The pride? The inflated ego? He did not fit into any mold! How would I destroy Him?

*What can be done with a man like the Teacher?* I asked the hounds of hell at our post-Sabbath conference. *Like Noah, He would not be silenced. Like Job, He trusts Creator. Like Daniel, He holds on to His beliefs at all cost. He must be destroyed! Destroyed! Destroyed! Destroyed*! I screamed over and over and over.

Then a glimmer of hope in the midst of my schemes after being totally shut down! The majority of the religious leaders scorned Him. He was not their "cup of tea." To them, His presence was as inconvenient as a fly in their precious ointment, not to be tolerated. Finally, a way in!

"Creator this; Creator that." Where had I heard those words before? And at every turn!

I studied His speeches, His manner of speaking. I observed His actions, His deeds, His miracles. I observed His attitude. I ascertained something. Oh, no! He could see into the spirit world! So that was one of His many secrets. How could He, being human, see into the realm of the spirit? I had to turn His "goodness" against Him. If He could see the supernatural, He might just instruct other humans to do so. Then my game would be up.

I got my wish! The foul smelling demons hissed in triumph. Fallen angels laughed in celebration. We had set a trap for the Teacher. One of His own sold Him out for money, thirty lousy pieces of silver. Very cheap, I might add. His betrayal was not even necessary for my trap.

Like it was at the time of His birth (*I finally figured out that it must have been the reason for all the angelic commotion*), there was unusual angelic activity. However, at this time, the angelic activity came from my side of the camp. Tempters—demons of despair, doubt, treachery, strife, greed, lust, fear, anger, hatred, malice, unbelief, selfishness—all were busy tormenting humans in the vicinity of the Teacher turned Rabbi. He was busy converting humans into Creator's kingdom. My hordes were busy ushering into hell as many as would yield to my forms of temptation. The wall of angels had come down, and I took advantage of the opportunity to steal, kill, and destroy.

I sprang the trap in a garden. Ha! Poetic injustice, wouldn't you say. A host of Creator's angels stood nearby, but they did not move. Was I lucky! I expected a battle I knew I could not win, but not one of the heavenly hosts raised his sword in the Rabbi's defense. Something was going on, but who cared? Victory was victory regardless of how it came about!

The capture of the Rabbi was sheer satanic ecstasy. I reviewed my list of tortures. What was the worst thing that could happen to this would-be Messiah? A dagger in His heart? Not bloody enough. Beheading? No, too quick. Poisoning? Too long. C-r-u-c-i-f-i-x-i-o-n. I considered humans stupid, but they followed my instruction to the "T" when it came down to murder.

*Beat Him! Hit Him harder and harder and harder! Rake into His flesh! Rip into His body. Scar Him! Maim Him! Draw blood! Degrade Him! Spit on Him! Rip off His clothes! Shame Him! Creator's Son?*

*Whip Him! Tear His face apart! Slash into His skull. Leave not one spot on His body unscathed! Then kill Him!*

The heavenly host stood motionless on the north side of the hill where the Rabbi had been taken. My hordes and I occupied the opposite side. My hordes had a shindig. They danced round and round. The air was flooded by legions after legions of demons and fallen angels. The horrid expressions on the faces of the demons were sights to behold. Evil spirits soared in and out of the circle of crucifixes. They yelled in the ears of the executioners, *More blood! More blood! Make the humans hurt; let the humans bleed!*

The dogs of hell flew over the heads of the women, especially that of His mother. They laughed and mocked the sadness and grief of the humans who surrounded the crosses. Although unable to make contact with the human forms in the natural realm, demons repeatedly and aimlessly pawed at the bodies of the humans standing below the crosses and at the bodies of the men on the crosses. Obscene gestures, lewd acts aimed at the humans were performed by the demon hordes. Humans had no clue of the debased spectacle that took place in the spirit world.

I resided over the event. I had no patience with the theatrics of demons and fallen angels. I feared the heavenly host that stood so solemn nearby. What if they were given an order to save the life of the Rabbi? I had ordered His death, so I wanted him dead before my order could be countermanded. My lust for blood was never satisfied, but we needed to kill Him quickly! Then and only then would I rejoice.

And so He died! And yet Creator's angels stood immobile. At His death, a powerful force shook the foundation of the Earth. The elements reacted, for the sun and moon exchanged places. The Earth became dark as night at three o'clock in the afternoon. The pit of hell was bathed in the light of the sun!

There He stood. I did not comprehend! He

stood in front of me. In the natural world, He was dead. The people handled His body. In the world of the supernatural, He stood right in front of me!

Do you know what He did? He literally snatched the key of hell from me and made His way into the place of the dead, a place where the spirits of the dead were kept.

No! This was not happening. I had known Him in Heaven, but I had not recognized Him in human form. Too late! I had orchestrated the death of the Son of Creator!

For His first thirty years, He walked the Earth, and I did not recognize Who He was! For another three years, I thought of Him as just another messiah wannabe. I had been duped into carrying out Creator's plans. Now I understood why Creator's angels had stood still while my servants killed Him! He was supposed to die. And I—I, the biggest fool of all time was used to fulfill the prophecy. Blood sacrifice? He was the blood sacrifice. What could I do? Absolutely nothing but watch.

His power became evident in the world of the spirits. He descended into hell, called out to the dead, and they answered. I watched like a wet rat, powerless to do anything, for I knew Who He was, and over Him, I had no power. One after the other, the souls of the dead cried out, declaring Creator as their Lord and Him as their Savior, for He had descended into the abyss to retrieve the souls of those who favored Creator. When He ascended back to Earth after three days, He emptied the pit. He took with Him the souls of the believing dead.

I thought He would never leave. I was exasperated, deflated, downcast, and downtrodden. The dogs of hell laughed at me. They roared and danced around me, poked fun at me, and dared me to follow Him upward. They dared me to attack.

*Attack? Attack?* I screamed. How dumb could one pack of demons be? Were their memories so short or their minds so dense that they did not remember the One they wanted me to challenge? We had lost the souls of those who sided with Creator. The episode that hell had experienced over the three-day period was merely a quiet battle!

However, the war was not over! There are millions and millions of humans just itching to be corrupted. My horde of fallen angels and demon spirits would do our utmost to kill them in the height of their corruption! I rallied my horde. They fell for my words, but then they always did. Stupid, stupid, stupid.

Again, the Earth was shaken with the force of an earthquake. Not my doing.

The demons informed me that He had returned to Earth in a restored body. I stayed my distance from Him. There was only one way I could hope to affect Him and His kingdom. Drag as many humans as I could into mine. Rather than follow Him around, I resumed my attack on the humans He loved enough to die for! I let Him do His own thing. Eventually, He went back to Heaven. Good riddance!

# CHAPTER XI

I am sick and tired of humans giving Creator credit for the murders and other vices I orchestrate. I steal, I kill, and I destroy, and I want my recognition for what I do.

I am a created being! I was made before the creation of mankind. I have seen the first man and woman, for I have been in the Garden of Eden. I did my best to mess up their lives, as I have tried and still try to destroy the lives of as many human beings as I can. Some humans have the audacity to believe that I consider them as friends. They even call themselves satan worshippers. Regardless, I have never been a true friend, never was, never will be, for I have chosen to hate everybody and every thing. What am I? A fallen angel that has mastered the art of deception. The epitome of all that is evil—that's me! A despicable, depraved, vile, base, deceitful, abominable, malevolent, immoral, corrupt, aberrant, and sinful fallen angel. I go by many names, the prince of darkness, Satan, the devil, and Beelzebub. A bona fide enemy of humanity is an appropriate description of me. A mere imposter, a pretender—thief, liar, deceiver, murderer—vile, sadistic fallen angel that has been kicked out of Heaven and cannot get permanent residency there ever again—a portrait of me.

A devil, a creature whose future will be eternal damnation—that's me.

I blame humans and Creator for any frustration I experience. First, I can never ever reside in Heaven. Who do you think gave the order to have me thrown out of Heaven in the first place? Currently, my home is in Earth's stratosphere, as close to Heaven as I will ever get. I travel to Heaven at times to make accusations against humans, but my visits are usually short.

Do you want to know what I plan to do to humans? Feather-brained, pampered group of know-nothings? I plan to steal, kill, and destroy everything that humans hold dear. I want birthrates slowed down or halted. If I can stop the reproductive process totally, that would be more to my liking. Since I cannot stop children from being born, I want to orchestrate the death of as many children as I can, either in the womb or while they are still young and innocent. I want children taken from their pathetic protective relatives and tortured, maimed, or murdered. If any should survive torture and mutilation, I want them forever dead inside. I want human offspring to have damaged consciences, broken spirits, and injured souls. It makes no difference to me which form death takes, as long as death happens, in one form or another. If I wipe out children, the fewer grow up to become adults. I want humans wiped from the face of this Earth!

I want humans to reject the existence of Creator and embrace the power of darkness. Humans who believe in the existence of Creator might do my kingdom harm. So I prefer to keep humans ignorant, even if it means they are ignorant of me.

Who is responsible for keeping humankind out of my clutches? Creator. I want to kill every human on planet Earth, but Creator keeps finding ways to keep them alive. If Creator had not made me, then I would not be in the dilemma I find myself. If Creator had not made humankind, then I would not be jealous and filled with envy of the relationship between Creator and His prized Creation.

Yes! Creator and humans, in my opinion, are responsible for my problems. Hence, I seek revenge on humankind to get back at Creator. With great vengeance, I carry on a mission to destroy His Creation. When I can, I steal all that humans have, kill whatever is dear to them, and as much as possible, destroy their dreams.

Humans are easy. Give them something valuable, and I can have their souls in exchange. An invention, a device, an answer to a scientific or medical question, and they become putty in my hands. They will argue the merits of the invention, the innovativeness of a device, or applaud answers to scientific or medical questions, but they will never question the source. They do not care about the source. Once they benefit or gain notoriety, why bother with learning anything else? They take credit and off they go. They are impressed with themselves. I understand their attitudes, for I impress myself too.

Daily, I hear many humans shouting praises

to Creator. I desperately want to steal His thunder, but I keep running into obstacles. Humans? Humans.

On Earth, I move up and down to see what humankind is up to. In my opinion, humans are always up to something. They are creative like the Creator, but they are too stupid to know this. Periodically, I come across humans who are stricken with chronic stubbornness, which I have labeled the "Job Factor," severe to chronic desire to serve Creator in a righteous manner. These become my primary targets!

What are my immediate plans for man's damnation? Attack all that humankind hold dear, corrupt everyone he loves, hinder his progress, alter his system of rules, and blind him to my devices, my modus operendi.

I copy; I cannot create. I kill; I cannot restore life. That's my whole purpose, to steal, kill, or destroy. I have chosen my current role! Just like you musty creatures called humans have free choice, so did I. And eons ago, I chose to be a liar, thief, and destroyer. I do my own thing. Unlike humans, however, fallen angels do not have the option to repent and start afresh. We are damned to hell, and we know it. We merely compensate by taking down as many humans as we can trick.

Many people do not understand how I can influence them. I put "hooks in the noses" of humans and pull them toward damnation. What are these hooks? Addictions! An addiction of any kind is a hook in the nose of the addicted, and he or she can be driven or pulled into evil by his or her addiction. When humans become addicted to any substance— food, drugs, alcohol, or sex, disembodied spirits might just have a chance to infiltrate that person's subconscious. What does being drunk do to the spirit? It opens up the doorway to the spirit world.

The first thing I do to undermine the human race is to steal everything I can from mankind. I steal their wisdom, knowledge, and understanding. Why should I have regard for mankind? In the end, humankind will choose me and my ways, debauchery, violence, sexual immorality.

Making humans afraid has been my focus since I was thrown out of Heaven. I want people to think that I am omnipresent, that I am everywhere at once.

I want humans to be wild—wilder than films portray so called prehistoric humans, wilder than any animal! Right now, I am doing a superb job on the current generation. So many are disrespectful to their parents and other adult figures; multitudes are unthankful, and most are unholy. I want these youngsters to grow up wild, without discipline and no natural affection—a generation to foster mayhem.

I am against young people abstaining from sexual intercourse until marriage; I am against monogamous relationships. If I have my way, the age of consent will be lowered to 12.

Actually, I've hated mankind since his creation. I have envied man's role in Creator's scheme of things. Creator made everything that you see for the baffled idiotic specimen called mankind. The sun, moon, stars—the seas, oceans and all that are in them—the animal and plant kingdoms—all created for the enjoyment and use of human beings. To think that Creator actually formed a stumbling, mumbling, error-prone, petty creature like a human being, dumber than the animals, just increases my hatred of humankind and my rage against all humans. Creator has done me an injustice by giving so much power and authority to humans who have no idea what to do with power. I am doing everything in my power (limited as it may be) to cause Creator's very own Creation to turn against Him. I have been practicing for years! Ha!

Humankind is hopeless. I lead them on a path to self-destruct. I am ready to see Creator's kingdom crumble!

So I have, since my eviction from Heaven, come down to Earth with a voluminous rage against and malicious hatred for humankind. My purpose is to turn them all from Creator so they, too, will be barred from Heaven. A Lake of Fire has been reserved for me where I'm damned to spend eternity. An eternity in a pit that burns with fire and brimstone is not an exciting future that I look forward to, so I plan to take with me to the pit of hell as many humans as I can.

What are my overall aims? I want to see humankind at his lowest—spiritually, financially, socially, physically, and emotionally. I want humans to conform to every decadent act, fad, or trend, and create their own forms of self-indulgent behaviors, each one worse than the first. I want each person to believe he or she is okay and needs no such thing as accountability to or forgiveness from anyone.

Dead relationships. If relationships can die, then I want to see the death of every relationship among humans. I want every man, woman, boy, and girl to passionately hate each other. I want every person on Earth to pass judgment continuously on everyone. I want every person the enemy of the other. I want families at odds continually, neighbors to harbor sweltering hatred for neighbors, and countries continually at war. I especially want to decimate or annihilate relationships among groups that declare that there is such a being as Creator.

I want to institute cycles of agony and defeat. I want to kill family members to multiply the number of bereaved, multiply pain and suffering of the sick, and devastate the poor and needy by making even bare necessities impossible to acquire. I want all humans to be impatient about everything, to be driven by evil spirits. I want humans to accept my words as truth and Creator's as fantasy. I want every human being that has ever lived to join my hordes of demons and me in the Lake of Fire that burns with brimstone. When the Book of Truth is opened and lifestyles are judged, I want to hear: Guilty! Guilty! Guilty!

What is my prognostication for the future? Changes, multiple changes.

Pornographic halls of worships. A pornographic theater placed in every neighborhood in place of Christian church. I will relish the day when majority of parents, without flinching, and their young children sit and watch pornographic videos on their television sets in their homes. Pornographic paraphernalia—posters, magazines, books, tapes— on sale in convenient stores, discount department stores, and all major grocery chains. Pornographic art classes will be electives in colleges and univer- sities and part of the day-to-day curriculum in high schools with corresponding porn textbooks.

Cannibalism will be the order of the day. The flesh of human beings sold as delicacies on the black market. The brain and heart being the most expen- sive, since there is so much ado about the "heart" of a human.

A new industry, the best yet—human organs on sale, not only to the very rich, but also to those of moderate income. Humans kept alive and penned as animals so organs or body parts can be removed to sell as these are ordered. With human organs for sale, imagine just how many humans will be abducted and killed just for body parts. No family member will be safe then. Can you imagine how many families will get rich at the expense of their children, husbands, or wives? Even grandparents will be at risk! The pow- erless and the weak will disappear totally!

Humans reduced to animalistic behavior. Rape, incest, bestiality, sodomy, lesbian coupling— openly on television, on the big screen, in backyards, on picnic grounds, on public beaches, or even on neighborhood sidewalks. No human even turns his or her head or looks the other way.

My best yet is the return of prayer to public schools. This time, however, prayers will be offered to any and all gods, those of the past and any new gods the populace can create. This will be the appropriate time for an exit from the closet of witches, warlocks, and satan worshipers.

What are my plans for humans? A new and improved desensitized human on the face of the Earth, until he brings about his own annihilation or the wrath of Creator.

I plan for morality to be removed from any semblance of godliness; that is, I want "right and wrong" to be totally orchestrated by the will of the people. The consensus of the majority will determine what is right or inappropriate. There will be no wrongness in any situation.

Take for instance, the issue of sex. Debauchery is in order. Human acceptance of incest and bestiality are primary on my list of priorities. I do not include homosexuality because tolerance and soon majority acceptance of men lying with men and women sleeping with women will soon be legislated. I have my agents at work trying to bring about the legislation that will make homosexuality a commonplace occurrence. With the acceptance and tolerance of homosexual lifestyles, legislation to accept incest and bestiality is forthcoming.

After homosexuality is firmly established as an acceptable lifestyle, then my imps will work on

the intellect of those who propagate incestuous relationships. Brothers and sisters, fathers and daughters, sons and mothers, sisters, brothers, cousins—all
coming together to create a sexual cesspool that only
demons can appreciate. Initially, the believers in Creator will denounce the move as diabolical. (How right
they are!) But a strong minority who wish to sanction
this deviant lifestyle will move to make sexual intercourse between family members an appropriate act,
not punishable by law. They will use the adage of
sexual preference and herald the relationship as an
"alternative family style." The sexual union of family
members will more than likely produce children who
might be deficient mentally, physically, and socially.

When humankind has plummeted to its lowest point because of acceptance of incest, then bestiality will be introduced; that is, laws will be introduced that will make it okay for humans to cohabit
with larger animals. First, it will be simply a matter
of privacy; that is, sex between humankind and larger
animals within a person's home will not be subject to
judgment by the law. However, those who become
consumed with this form of sexual perversion will
seek the world's approval by chanting "an alternative human-animal lifestyle." Justification? The act
would improve relations between the "human and
animal kingdoms." The consenting minority, though
small, will try to exert pressure on the disapproving
majority by screaming, *Intolerance*! Many who dis-
approve will re-think their stance, suffer from a guilt
complex, and will refuse to either speak against bes-

tiality or sanction the act. After the practice becomes open and accepted by a recognizable majority, then laws will be passed to sanction sexual intercourse between humankind and animals.

To further desensitize the public, scene of men and women engaged in sexual acts with the animals of their preference will be included in prime time television shows and in movies. Parents and their children (if children are still being produced at this point) will sit in front of television sets or movie screens and view sitcoms or movies that hint at or show scenes of human-animal sexual encounters. From man's union with animals, there will be no procreation. Thus, I will have driven another stake in God's command to be "fruitful, multiply and fill the Earth." Human reproduction will be at an all time low. My hordes and I will have taken the race of humans down to the status of beasts. How can I predict these things? I have had eons to study the actions and attitudes of humankind. This is how they do it!

# EPILOGUE

There are no special rehabilitative programs for fallen angels. I cannot repent. I can never again live in the presence of Creator, so I hate all who has that possibility to do so.

What are my immediate goals? Corrupt each present generation; hinder their ability to pro-create. Influence humans to legislate morality. Convince humankind that there is no such being as Creator. Turn the affections of humankind "inward" and promote sexual promiscuity and sexual experimentation.

I would like to count on twenty-first-century humans to assist me in carrying out my plans. Yet, I cannot count on these to do my bidding, because deep in the heart of supposedly "liberated societies," many humans have deep rooted senses for doing the "right" thing. Their propensity to do this "right thing" during my prime time causes havoc in the kingdom of darkness. Just when I think the Earth is mine, humans band together to perpetrate kind acts to other humans or cities or nations. Humans are so inconsistent!

For example, for most of the twentieth century, the stronghold on nations was discrimination. The populace had no clue that they were instruments in a satanic war waged from hell to foster prejudice, segregation, and racial cleansing. I had every demon of strife and dissemination actively moving about nations to keep the war ongoing. What do some busybody humans do? Wage a worldwide struggle against apartheid. The struggle made me look bad in the world of the spirits. I am still striving to salvage what is left of strongholds of racial discrimination.

I have been working to steal, kill, and destroy humankind for the past six thousand years. I walked through the Garden of Eden, presided at the Tower of Babel, and experimented in Sodom and Gomorrah. I inspired the use of slave labor at slavery's inception through the building of pyramids around the globe, the enslavement of the Hebrews in Egypt, slavery throughout the Roman and Grecian periods, the Africa to America saga, slavery in countries of Africa today, and many other so-called "secret" slavery rings. I levitated in the arenas while Christians were being eaten by lions, and I roared with laughter while Nero's fires burned within inches of destroying Rome. The Bubonic plague in Europe was a satanic filler. I prided myself during the backward thrust in learning during the Middle Ages when someone suggested that humans should learn to read. Barbarianism, cannibalism—I have had my hands in every bloody war or act that killed humans since the inception of time, including human sacrifices by ancient people, religious persecutions as well. The witch hunts in Europe and the Americas were strategic, if I do say so myself. Famine, conflicts, and wars—massacres, homicide, infanticide, suicide, genocide—any act of human destruction, I participated in. I did not cause them all, but when the opportunity presented itself, I joined in to make matters as worst as the situations could get!

How do I do all of this? Through branding suggestions into human minds. A being as powerful as I, who has been around for as long as I have, can surely outdo the local psychic or hypnotist! I reach most humans through their minds, their intellect. When the mind is pliable and willing to allow demonic infiltration, then demons move in! Then I have control of that human. Unless . . . but let's not talk about that now.

Overall, for nearly six thousand years, I have wreaked havoc among and against mankind, yet my overall success ratio has been fair to moderate. Always there was a "savior" of some kind—a prophet here, a saint there—someone to enlighten humankind that evil truly exist, and that they should look to and serve Creator to avoid being engulfed in my specialty: unadulterated corruption.

It was about two thousand years ago, give or take a few years, when I sensed that Earth was "ripe" for something new and different. I have orchestrated the deaths of judges, prophets, kings, missionaries, and pastors. I indirectly organized cults, orders, sects, and religions. I have manipulated rulers, kings, fallen angels, and demons to do my biddings. I have devised plots, takeovers, and wars. I have manufactured famines and disasters, natural and man-made. Then He came on the scene. He was like no human

I had ever tempted. I had come so close to conquest only to experience total defeat!

How do humans view the world where I reside? Most humans do not consider it at all! I sit in galleries and country clubs of the supposedly "sophisticated" where I hear them discuss the world of the spirit as tribal nonsense of the ignorant, the downtrodden, and the poor. In pool halls, pubs, barbershops, beauty salons, and other human haunts, I hear humans speak of misfortunes and bad luck.

I vie for ownership of the souls of humans, and whether humans believe it or not, my hordes and I constantly battle with the angelic host of Heaven over the souls of humans. Humans' freedom to choose between Creator's kingdom and mine is the cause of angelic confrontations. I want to command the world, both the invisible and the visible; for I have seized control of the minds of so many humans that society seems to favor me over Creator.

I was forewarned in the Garden of retribution. I have known since then that my undoing would come by way of a human, one like the very ones I have spent most of my existence trying to conquer or wipe out. I was forewarned that a male of the human race would bring about my defeat and an end to my evil kingdom. How did I know all of this? Unlike most of you, I read. Whenever I want to know what is happening in the realm of humans, I check the Scriptures. I read the words and I read between the lines.

If I am destined to go down, I plan to go down

with a bang! I plan to take the downward plunge with as many humans as I can carry. So humans, "Beware!"

In the meantime . . .

Contact A. E. Hepburn
or order more copies of this book at

TATE PUBLISHING, LLC

127 East Trade Center Terrace
Mustang, Oklahoma 73064

(888) 361 - 9473

Tate Publishing, LLC

www.tatepublishing.com